BOWLS

(Crown & Flat Green)

PLAY·THE·GAME

BOWLS

(Crown & Flat Green)

Barry Weekes ·

Ward Lock Limited · London

First published in Great Britain in 1988
by Ward Lock Limited, 8 Clifford Street,
London W1X 1RB, an Egmont Company

Senior Editor Ian Morrison

Designed by Anita Ruddell

Illustrations by Peter Bull Art

Text set in Helvetica
by Hourds Typographica, Stafford, England
Printed and bound in Great Britain
by Richard Clay Ltd, Bungay, Suffolk

British Library Cataloguing in Publication Data

Weekes, Barry
    Play the game : bowls (crown & flat green).
    1. Bowling on the green
    I. Title
    796.31   GV909

    ISBN 0–7063–6660–3

Acknowledgments

The author and publishers would like to
thank Mr R. Holt, Secretary of the British
Crown Green Bowling Association, and
Mr F. J. Inch, Assistant Secretary of the
English Bowling Association.

Thanks are also due to Colorsport, who
supplied the photographs reproduced in this
book.

Frontispiece: **David Bryant – twice World
Outdoor Champion, three times World
Indoor Champion and, not surprisingly, the
best-known player on the scene!**

CONTENTS

FOREWORD

It was a great pleasure to accept the publisher's request to write a short foreword to this publication, especially as the book refers to the game of bowls in general and does not refer only to one particular code. A number of books have been written about the game of bowls, but most of them relate exclusively to the flat green code; too few, regrettably, deal in a comprehensive manner with the 'other' code of bowls – Crown Green. This particular publication covers all aspects of both Crown and Flat Green Bowls and serves as a first class introduction to a magnificent and popular game, whatever your choice of code.

After providing a comprehensive history of bowls, the author deals with the equipment necessary to play the game. I am sure that the bowls beginner will not have previously realized how different the Flat and Crown Green games are, but he will soon appreciate the tremendous differences when he first compares the equipment used. The techniques required to play the two games are once again as different as chalk and cheese, but at least the explanatory notes on this subject will enable the aspiring bowler to make the choice to suit himself.

Normally, just to read and digest the rules of any game can be quite an ordeal, but *Play the Game: Bowls* is written with the beginner in mind and the author makes the rules of both games extremely easy to follow and fully understand.

Play the Game: Bowls is a most welcome publication on our sport. I sincerely hope that many people, of all ages and who have never before played the game, read it, understand it, take up bowls and enjoy every minute of their new pastime. My sincere thanks to the author for taking the time to write such a useful book.

Ron Holt
Secretary of the British Crown Green Bowling Association

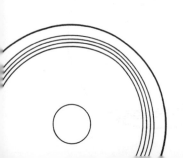

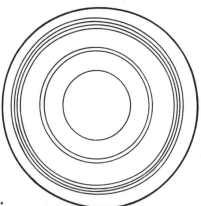

FOREWORD

Bowls has long since lost its image of being an old man's game. Happily, rinks up and down the country are occupied by youngsters, who are the potential international players and champions of the future. But where should they start? Guiding newcomers in any sport is never an easy task. Just how far do you go when trying to teach them the rules of the game, the basic skills and so on? However, Ward Lock, with their new series *Play the Game,* have come up with the ideal blend.

Play the Game: Bowls is one of the best books ever produced for the newcomer to flat green bowls, and the instruction and information is well condensed in an easy to read and understandable manner, without insulting the intelligence of the reader. You are guided through the complete game of flat green bowls, from the basics of the game to an interesting 'Rules Clinic', which will answer all those most often-asked queries. Bowls equipment is covered in detail and the most important rules of all, those of etiquette, are fully explained. Basic skills, and how to play those awkward shots, are detailed, but

as compiler Barry Weekes rightly says, the best way to learn the game is by spending many hours – and hopefully happy hours – out on the rink.

In addition to all this, there is much in this book for those of you who have been playing the game for a while; you will find the opening chapter on the history of bowls fascinating, as you are guided through time from the day Sir Francis Drake immortalized our great game at Plymouth Hoe to the present day of television and commercialized bowls.

I hope you enjoy reading this book as much as we have at the English Bowling Association. For all you youngsters taking up bowls, there can be no finer starting place than *Play the Game.*

R. Stapleton
President of the English Bowling Association

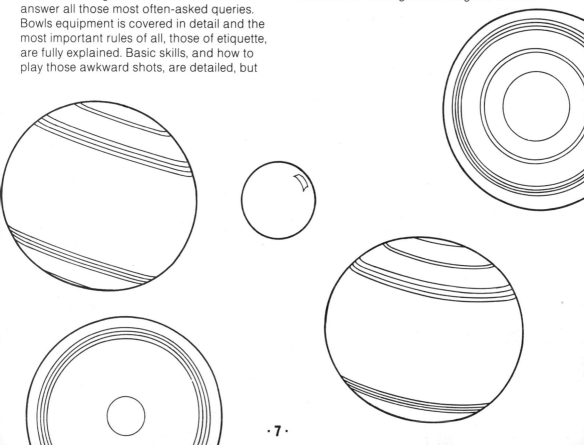

HISTORY &
DEVELOPMENT OF
BOWLS

Many sports can trace their origins to early civilizations and bowls is certainly no exception – historians have discovered that the ancient Egyptians played a form of the game more than 7000 years ago. It was not until the thirteenth century, however, that bowls was first recorded as being a game of delicate skills with the object of the game to get the bowl nearer to another target. It is generally accepted that the object of earlier variations was to *hit* the target.

The Southampton Bowls Club is reputed to be the oldest club in the world, its lawn having been laid in 1187. The green came into regular use in 1299 and the club still promotes a tournament each year to celebrate that first tournament. The Chesterfield Bowling Club, however, claims a rink dating to 1294.

In the early fourteenth century, Edward III, who was intent on making sure the bowmen of England had their archery practice, banned the playing of bowls, just as he did other sports. Despite the edicts put on the game for nearly 500 years, it still became very popular and in the sixteenth century bowls with intentional bias were introduced, possibly by Charles Brandon, known as the Duke of Suffolk. In this way a new element of skill was added to the game.

If any sport has gained publicity from a single event in world history then that sport is bowls. On 19 July 1588 Sir Francis Drake was playing bowls at Plymouth Hoe. On being told the Spanish Armada had been sighted he refused to leave the bowls lawn until his game was complete: 'There is plenty of time to win this game *and* thrash the Spaniards too', Drake is reputed to have said.

The first notable set of rules of bowls was drawn up by Charles II in 1670. The game also became very popular in Scotland and in the mid-nineteenth century a committee was drawn up to formulate a code of laws. The job was given to Glasgow solicitor, W. W. Mitchell, whose code was accepted and has remained almost unaltered ever since. The Scots were responsible for developing flat greens and for taking the game overseas.

The Scottish Bowling Association was formed in 1892 but the English Bowling Association (EBA) was not formed until June 1903 with test cricketer W. G. Grace, a keen bowls player, as its first president. The first

The increasingly popular variation of indoor bowls, the short mat game. It is played on a mat 6ft (1·84m) wide and either 45, 30 or 24ft (13·5, 9 or 7·2m) long. To make play more difficult, and skilful, you have to bowl around a wooden block (known as the 'windmill'), which is placed in the centre of the mat.

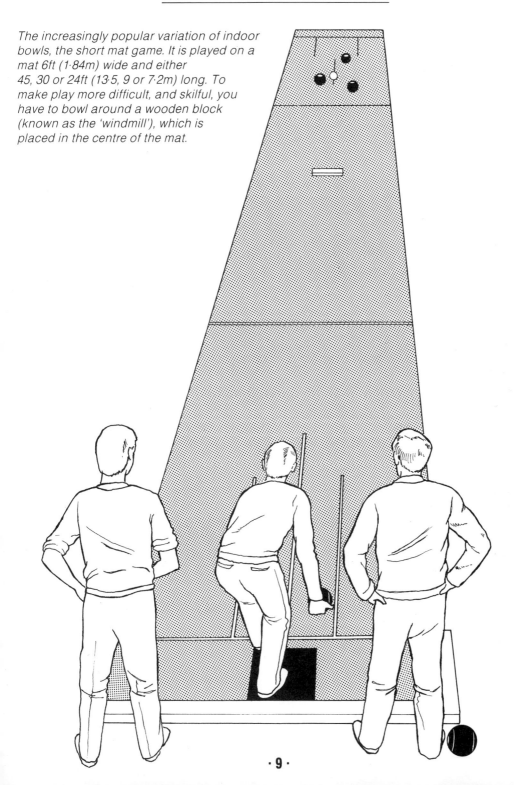

BOWLS

Scottish Championships were in 1894 while the inaugural English Championships were not until eleven years later.

As the game spread throughout the world it necessitated the formation of a world governing body and in July 1905 the International Bowling Board (IBB) was formed in Cardiff. It succeeded the Imperial Bowling Association which had been formed to arrange matches between Commonwealth countries, and in 1930 bowls was included in the first Commonwealth Games at Hamilton, Canada. It has been included in every Games since, except 1966 when the first World Championships were held.

The English Bowling Federation (EBF) was formed in 1945 because there were some counties, predominantly in the Midlands and the North, who preferred to play their own variation and did not want to be controlled by the rules as laid down by the EBA. Both are, however, flat green games.

Women have been playing bowls since the turn of the century, and in 1931 the English Women's Bowling Association was formed following the efforts of the 'Mother of English Women's Bowling', Clara Johns.

The indoor game, very popular today, was pioneered by W. G. Grace during his term as EBA president; although the Scot William Macrea demonstrated indoor bowls on a concrete floor covered with sawdust at Drumdryan, Scotland, in 1888, Grace was responsible for laying out a carpet at the Crystal Palace. The first indoor club is believed to have been formed at Edinburgh's Synod Hall in 1905 when members of the Edinburgh Winter Bowling Association was formed and members played on two 27-yard gaslit rinks, so indoor bowls is not a new innovation as many believe.

The English Indoor Bowling Association was formed in 1933 but only as the Indoors Section of the EBA. It was granted autonomy in 1971, and in 1979 the first indoor World Championships were held.

Following the growth in popularity of indoor bowls, it is now an all-the-year-round sport, and more indoor centres are being built to cater for the increase in demand.

Throughout this book we will be looking at the rules and techniques of Lawn Bowls (also known as Flat Green Bowls), both indoor and outdoor as governed by the IBB and the EBA, as well as Crown Green Bowls.

Crown Green bowls is played mostly in the North and Midlands of England, North Wales, and the Isle of Man, and gets its name because the centre of the green is higher than its boundaries and is believed to have evolved from the inability to produce flat level greens in many of the industrial areas of the north. Most greens are adjacent to public houses, and betting, among players and spectators, is a common feature of the Crown Green game, unlike the tea and home-made cakes atmosphere of Lawn bowls.

Earliest reference to the Crown Green game dates to the 1870s, but it was not until 1888 that the game's first administrative body, the Lancashire and Cheshire Association, was formed. The governing body, the British Crown Green Bowling Association (BCGBA) was founded in 1907 as the National Amateur Crown Green Bowling Association. The word 'amateur' was dropped in 1972. The new body brought together the County Associations which had been formed at the turn of the century.

The game originally catered only for the amateur. Prize money was strictly forbidden. Professional players did exist however, and they formed their own Professional Players Association, known as the 'Panel'. They used to play daily matches arranged at venues in the heart of Crown Green land: Lancashire. The games were 41-up and betting was an important feature of Panel games. They still exist today, but Panel games are not as well

Indoor bowls is becoming increasingly popular all over the country, particularly the space-saving short mat variety.

supported as they used to be and games tend to be 31-up instead of 41.

The paying of prize money caused friction within Crown Green bowling circles and the Lancashire Association was expelled from the parent association for failing to suspend players who contravened the rules regarding playing for money. With the game going open in 1972, the amateur player ceased to exist.

Crown Green bowling has grown in popularity since the early 1970s and the number of County Associations has risen from ten to fifteen. The game is now spreading from its traditional roots in Lancashire to surrounding counties. There is even a crown green in the heart of Flat Green land, at Bournemouth. Suddenly the Dorset town has become a popular holiday venue with northern Crown Green bowlers!

A lot of Crown Green tournaments are handicap events. The game's top tournament, played annually at Blackpool's Waterloo Hotel, is the Waterloo Handicap – the most sought after trophy in the sport.

Because of the nature of its green, the Crown Green game is rarely played indoors. However, there is one indoor Crown Green bowling centre in England, at Birkenhead, Merseyside. There are, however, many professional indoor tournaments on the flat surface which bring together the best players from both codes to display their talents. Crown Green players tend to adapt to playing on flat green surfaces better than in a vice versa situation.

A recent innovation has been the introduction of a short mat game, so called because it is played on a narrow mat and is ideal for playing in confined spaces. Many snooker halls and sports clubs are installing short mat bowling strips. To add to the skill a wooden block (known as a 'windmill') is situated half way up the mat and the bowlers have to bowl around it thus providing a deterrent against striking. It is a popular game amongst Crown Green bowlers in the winter months.

Bowls is a game that is rapidly increasing in popularity and the fact that more indoor bowling centres have opened means it is now an all-the-year-round sport. Television coverage of the major tournaments has helped and the amount of sponsorship now finding its way into bowls can only be good for its long term future.

The game's popularity thrives on the fact that it induces friendships; players in both codes are encouraged to address their opponent(s) by their first names. Other reasons for the game's success are the facts that age is no barrier and both sexes can compete against each other on equal terms.

The fact that bowls is not an expensive game to play helps its popularity. You do not even have to invest in your own bowls initially, as these can be hired for a nominal charge from your local municipal park. If you are playing regularly, and particularly in Britain, a good set of waterproofs is, however, a wise investment!

No matter which form of bowls you play, you will soon learn that it is a game of delicate skill and tact. It is also a game that generates much warmth and sportsmanship; that is one of the successes of bowls as a participant and spectator sport. The image of bowls being an 'old man's game' has long gone. To reach the top at bowls these days you need to start young. Hopefully this book will provide a good starting point for the young player.

EQUIPMENT &
TERMINOLOGY

Before starting to learn how to play bowls, it is important to familiarize yourself with the equipment needed, and the terminology you will encounter during a game. Throughout the book we will be looking at the three most popular forms of bowls; Flat Green (Lawn), Indoor, and Crown Green Bowls.

EQUIPMENT –
FLAT · GREEN · BOWLS · (OUTDOOR)

The green

The Green should form a square of not less than 40yd (36·58m) and not more than 44yd (40·23m). The surface should be level and

The standard green

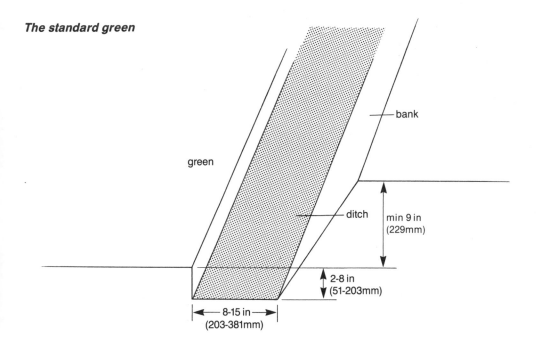

bank

green

ditch

min 9 in
(229mm)

2-8 in
(51-203mm)

8-15 in
(203-381mm)

BOWLS

The ditch

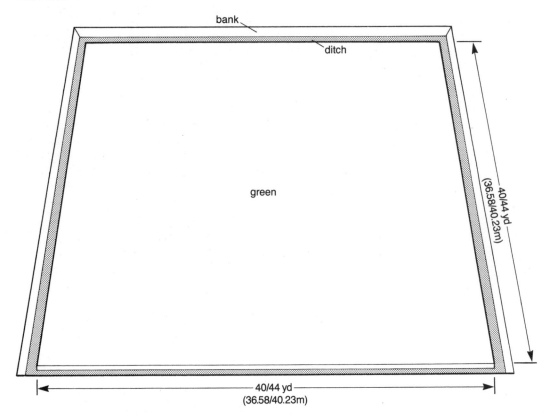

bank

ditch

green

40/44 yd
(36.58/40.23m)

40/44 yd
(36.58/40.23m)

the playing area should be surrounded with suitable boundaries in the form of a ditch and a bank.

The ditch should be not less than 8in (203mm) nor more than 15in (381mm) wide and shall not be less than 2in (51mm) or more than 8in (203mm) below the level of the green. The bottom of the ditch should be of a surface unlikely to cause any damage to the bowls and, of course, it should be free of any impediment or article likely to cause damage to the bowl.

The top of the bank at the back of the ditch should be not less than 9in (229mm) above the level of the green and either upright or at an angle of not more than 35° from the perpendicular. The surface of the bank, like the ditch, should be of a surface not likely to cause damage to the bowls.

Rinks

The green shall be divided into equal spaces, called rinks, and they should be no more than 19ft (5·79m) or less than 18ft (5·48m) wide. The confine of each rink is marked by placing pegs at the four corners. Thread is pulled tightly between the corner pegs to run the full length of the rink. Each rink is numbered consecutively and the centre of each rink is indicated by positioning a peg or other suitable marker on the bank at each end of the rink.

The above dimensions are those laid

The bank

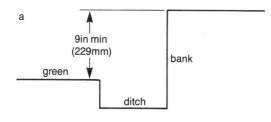

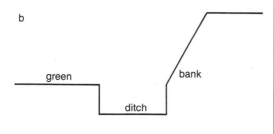

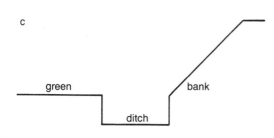

Of these three banks, A and B are legal but C, because its angle is greater than 35 degrees, is not.

down by the International Bowling Board. National Associations can make their own variations and the EBA, for example, stipulate square greens measuring 44yd (40·23m) maximum and 33yd (30·17m) minimum. Rectangular greens are also permitted with the longer side restricted to a maximum 44yd (40·23m) and the shorter side not less than 33yd (30·17m). For domestic use the greens may be divided into rinks of not less than 14ft (4·27m) or more than 19ft (5·79m). Boundary threads are not compulsory under the EBA rules.

The bowls

Bowls are made of wood (Lignum Vitae), rubber or composition and shall be black or brown in colour. Although some players still prefer wooden bowls, the composition bowl is the more popular these days. Because all bowls were originally made of wood, bowls are still often referred to as 'woods'. The maximum diameter of wooden bowls shall be $5\frac{1}{4}$in (133mm) and $4\frac{5}{8}$in (117mm) and not exceed 3lb 8oz (1·59kg) in weight. The loading of bowls is strictly prohibited. The size of rubber or composition bowls is the same as above except that the maximum diameter is $5\frac{1}{8}$in (130mm). The average player uses a wood weighing 3lb $5\frac{3}{4}$oz (1·52kg) and with a 5in (127mm) diameter.

The above sizes are those laid down by the IBB for use in international matches. National and local associations permit variations from those dimensions.

In major competitions, each player has to distinguish his own bowl with some distinctive marking for identification purposes.

For a further detailed description of bowls and how the bias affects the run of a bowl see page 35.

The jack

The jack is the object ball to which players attempt to get at least one bowl nearer than those of their opponent(s). It is round and white with a diameter of not less than $2\frac{15}{32}$in (63mm) and not more than $2\frac{17}{32}$in (64mm). Its weight shall not be less than 8oz (227gm) or more than 10oz (283gm). It does not have a bias. Every game of bowls begins with the delivery of the jack.

BOWLS

Rinks

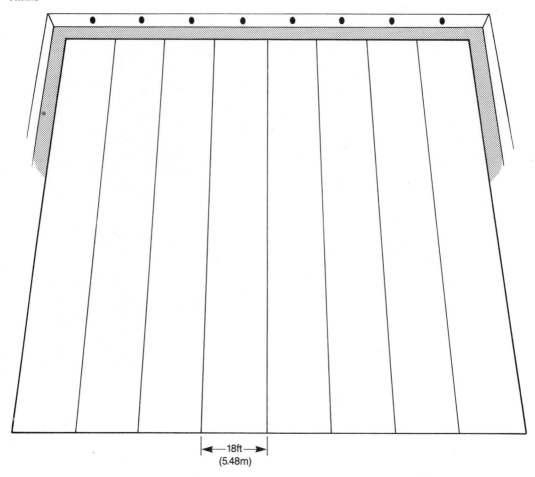

|←— 18ft —→|
(5.48m)

How a 48yd (20·23m) square green would be divided into eight rinks, each 18ft (5·48m) wide. Note the markers on the bank to indicate the middle of the rink.

A complete set of four lawn bowls. All four must be the same size, weight and have the same bias. If you look closely at the bottom of bowl A, you will see how it has been shaped more on one side to create the bias.

EQUIPMENT · & · TERMINOLOGY

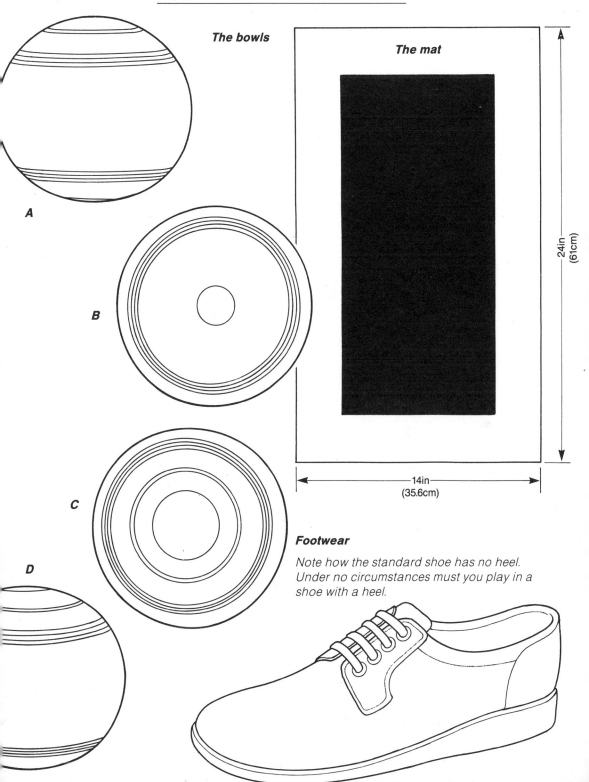

The bowls

A

B

C

D

The mat

24in
(61cm)

├── 14in ──┤
(35.6cm)

Footwear

Note how the standard shoe has no heel. Under no circumstances must you play in a shoe with a heel.

The mat

The mat, on which a player takes his stance before delivering his bowl, is rectangular and is 24in (61cm) long and 14in (35·6cm) wide. It is normally made of rubber.

Footwear

Players, umpires and markers must wear white, brown or black, smooth-soled, heel-less footwear while on the green. One of the biggest crimes in bowling is walking across the green with heeled shoes . . . so no stiletto heels on the green.

The EBA stipulate that brown-only footwear must be worn.

EQUIPMENT –
FLAT · GREEN · BOWLS · (INDOOR)

The principal differences between the equipment for indoor bowls and the outdoor game concern the playing surface, and the jack.

The size of **the green** shall form a rectangle or square of not less than 35yd (32m) and not more than 44yd (40m) in length and with a minimum width of 15ft (4·57m). The laws of the game do not stipulate what material the indoor surface should be made out of but, like the outdoor game, stipulates that the surface shall be level. A **ditch** is required at the two ends of the rink.

The **division of the green (rinks)**, like the outdoor game, must not be more than 19ft (5·79m) but the minimum width is considerably smaller for the indoor game, at 12ft (3·6m).

In indoor bowls the **jack** is a slightly different size, but considerably heavier. The diameter should be not less than $2\frac{15}{32}$in (63mm) and not more than $2\frac{21}{32}$in (66·6mm), which is similar to a jack in the outdoor game, but the weight is considerably heavier with a minimum of $13\frac{1}{2}$oz (382gm) and a maximum of 16oz (453gm). The maximum weight for a jack in outdoor bowls is 10oz (283gm).

Apart from the changes outlined above, the two games are virtually the same. The mat is the same size, and the bowls used for the indoor game are the same as in their outdoor counterpart.

And now for something different . . .

EQUIPMENT –
CROWN · GREEN · BOWLS

While the rules governing the equipment of indoor and outdoor Flat Green bowls as outlined are similar, those governing the

A crown green

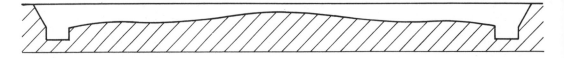

A cross-section of a crown green could look something like this. The crown at the centre can be as high as 18ft (4·57m) above the sides.

Several matches in progress in an indoor bowls hall.

Crown Green game are different from the other two, and if you are to specialize in this form of bowls, it is advisable to forget most of what you read on the foregoing pages, and start here.

The green

The British Crown Green Bowling Association makes no reference to the dimensions of the green in their Laws of the Game. Because of the differences in surfaces, all of which contain their own irregularities, it is impossible to define a Crown Green Bowling Green. In general they are 40yd (36·6m) square with a crown at the middle which can be anything from 6–18in (152–457mm) higher than the sides. The green does not have to be surrounded by a ditch because it does not play the same role in Crown Green Bowls as in the Flat Green game. Most crown greens do have ditches, however, to stop wayward bowls. The entrance to the green should be at or near the centre of one of the sides and clearly

marked. Crown greens are not divided into rinks because the jack can be played to any part of the green.

The bowls

Standard bowls as defined on page 15 are used. Although, once again, the Laws of Crown Green bowling do not lay down any regulations concerning the bowls.

The Crown Green bowler normally uses lighter bowls than his Flat Green rival and will often have a couple of sets, a smaller set for use on a fast green and a bigger set for use on a slower green.

As the jack is biased in Crown Green bowls, and to a standard bias of 2, most bowlers choose a set of bowls with a similar bias. The average male Crown Green bowler, with normal-sized hands, will play with a bowl weighing 2lb 12oz (1·25kg) and with a diameter of $4\frac{13}{16}$in (122·5mm).

The jack

The jack in Crown Green bowls is considerably different from that in Flat Green bowls. For a start, its size and weight are much greater and, unlike its Flat Green counterpart, it has a bias. The standard jack has a number 2 bias and is approved by the British Crown Green Bowling Association and stamped accordingly. For jacks stamped before October 1987, their weight should fall within a minimum of 20oz (567gm) and maximum 23oz (652gm). For those stamped after that date, the minimum weight shall be 21oz (595gm) and maximum

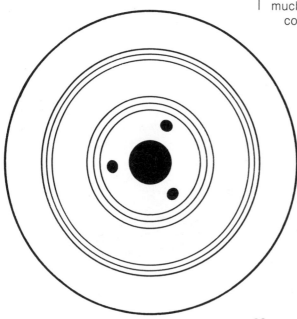

Crown green jack

This shows the non-biased side of the jack.

24oz (680gm). The diameter of the jack, both before and after October 1987, shall be $3\frac{1}{4}$in (95mm) minimum and $3\frac{7}{8}$in (98mm) maximum. The jack is either black or white, and three spots, in the form of a triangle, shall be marked on the non-biased side of the jack. You must always be told by, or tell, your opponent with which bias the jack has been delivered. Assessing the line of delivery will be impossible otherwise.

The footer

The footer is the equivalent of the mat in Flat Green bowls. The rules governing the footer are more specific than those governing the use of the mat in the Flat Green game.

Correct delivery

The rules categorically state that every player must place his toe on the footer when delivering a jack or bowl. A player delivering the jack with his right hand must play his bowls with his right hand and must have his

A correct and legitimate delivery, with the right hand and with the right foot on the footer.

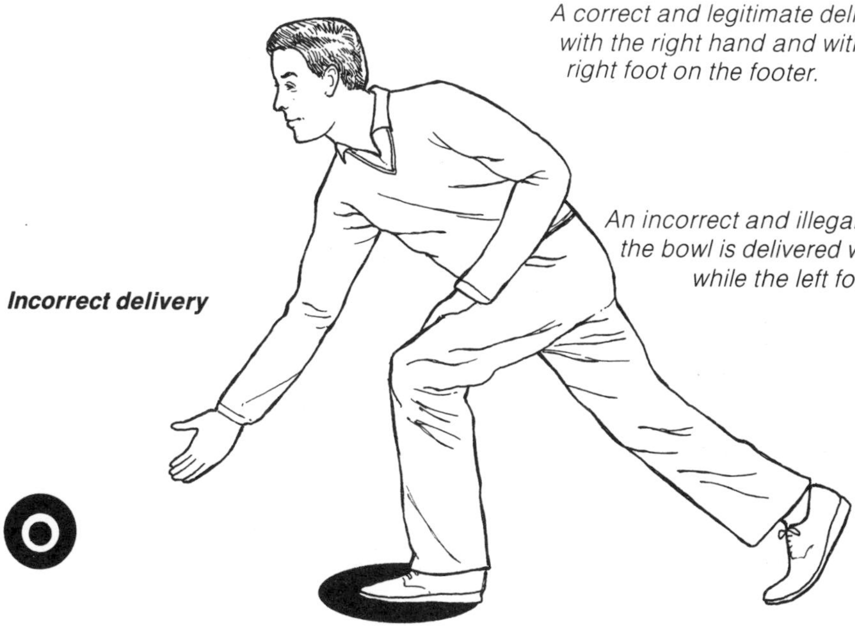

An incorrect and illegal delivery, because the bowl is delivered with the right hand while the left foot is on the footer.

Incorrect delivery

right toe on the footer at the time of delivery. The same applies in reverse in the case of a left-handed bowler. These rules do not apply in the case of disabled bowlers.

The footer, normally made of rubber, is round (the mat is rectangular in Flat Green bowls). Its diameter should be not less than 5in (128mm) or more than 6in (154mm).

Footwear

Crown Green bowling is not as definitive in its rules about footwear as its Flat Green counterpart but does insist that leather hard- or block-heeled footwear should NOT be worn on the green. Obviously, any heeled shoes are going to cause damage to the playing surface and flat-soled shoes are to be worn at all times.

Right, we are nearly ready to get down to learning the basics of bowls, but first of all some terminology.

TERMINOLOGY –
FLAT · GREEN · BOWLS
(OUTDOOR & INDOOR)

Backhand   The delivery of a bowl that travels towards the jack from a left-handed direction, i.e. the bias is on the right-hand side of the bowl (vice versa for left-handed players).

Block (or guard)   A bowl resting in the line of draw, or in front of the jack, thus hindering an opponent's shot.

Bowl in course   The term for a bowl from the moment of its delivery until it comes to rest.

Cot   Another name for the jack.

Covered   When the jack or a bowl is guarded by another bowl in front of it.

Backhand

The backhand shot *is played from left-to-right and with the bias on the right-hand side of the bowl.*

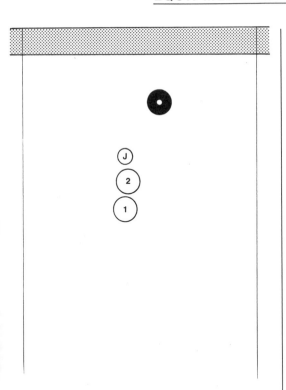

Covered

In this head the jack is covered by bowl no 2, which is in turn covered by no 1.

Dead bowl   A bowl is dead if:
  (a) it comes to rest in the ditch (unless it is a toucher);
  (b) it rebounds on to the rink after hitting the bank, or striking a toucher or jack in the ditch;
  (c) if it comes to rest within 15yd (13·71m) of the front of the mat;
  (d) if after completing its course, or as a result of further play, it comes to rest outside the boundaries of the rink.

Dead end   An end is deemed to be dead if the jack is dead. The jack is dead when it has been driven off the green and comes to rest outside the boundary of the rink. All dead ends shall be replayed in the same

Forehand

The opposite of the backhand shot, the forehand is played from right-to-left with the bias on the left-hand side of the bowl.

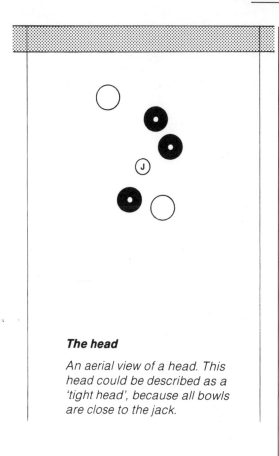

The head

An aerial view of a head. This head could be described as a 'tight head', because all bowls are close to the jack.

'Jack high'

Bowl B is said to be 'jack high'.

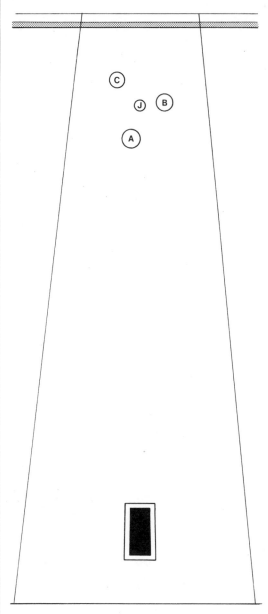

direction (unless both skips agree otherwise) and the delivery of the jack is retained by the player who delivered it initially.

Drive   A drive is a bowl delivered with force and with the intention of breaking up the head.

End   An end comprises the playing of the jack and all bowls by all players in the same direction on the rink.

Fast green   A green may be fast because it has been cut short or has dried out in sunny conditions. A bowl will take a wider curve and longer course on a fast green.

EQUIPMENT · & · TERMINOLOGY

Live bowls

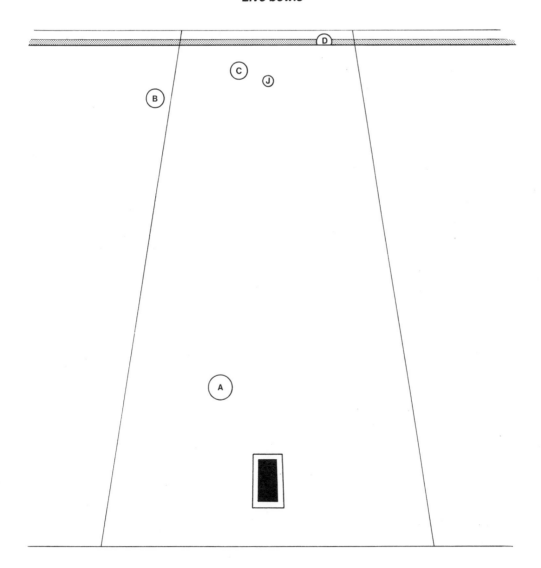

Only Bowl C is a live bowl. Bowl B is not, *because it has come to rest outside the rink. Bowl D is also a 'dead' bowl because it has come to rest in the ditch (assuming it did not become a 'toucher' by hitting the jack first), and Bowl A is dead because it has not travelled at least 15yd (13.71m) from the front of the mat.*

BOWLS

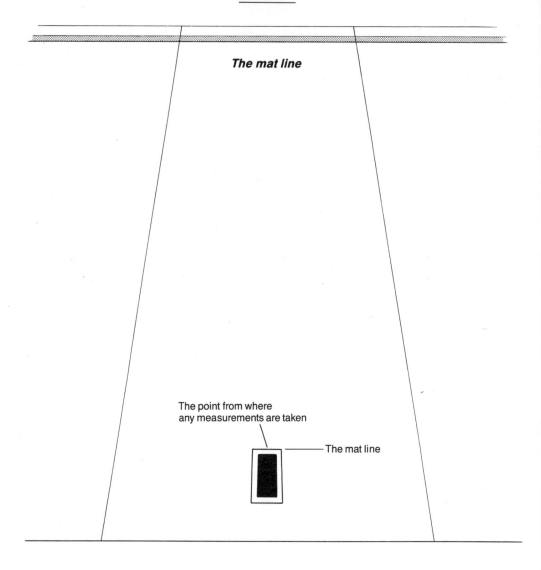

The mat line

The point from where
any measurements are taken

The mat line

Forehand   The delivery of a bowl that will travel towards the jack from a right-handed direction, with the bias on the left-hand side of the bowl (vice versa for left-handed players).

Four   A team consisting of four men. In order of play they are named: the lead, second, third, and skip. Each player delivers two bowls only.

Head.   The head is the name given to the jack and all bowls that have come to rest on the rink, provided that they are not dead.

Jack high   A ball is said to be jack high when the nearest part of it is equidistant from the mat as the nearest part of the jack to the mat.

Kitty   Another name for the jack.

Live bowl   Any ball that travels at least 15yd (13·71m) from the front edge of the mat, and legitimately comes to rest within the boundaries of the rink, is a live bowl.

Marker   The marker plays an important role in a game of bowls. His duties are:

(a) to control the game in accordance with the laws;
(b) to check that all bowls comply with legal requirements before the commencement of a game;
(c) to ascertain the width of the rink before the start of a game;
(d) to position the jack in the centre of the rink, and in the case of a full length jack ensure that it is 2yd (1·84m) from the ditch;
(e) to ensure that the jack is at least 70ft (21·35m) (under EBA rules this is 25yd (22·86m)) from the front of the mat when centred;
(f) to indicate to any player the approximate distance of any bowl from the jack or from another bowl. If required he shall measure any doubtful shots upon completion of the end but, if unable to come to a decision, must call for the assistance of the umpire;
(g) to mark all touchers with chalk;
(h) to mark the scorecard at the completion of each end and keep the players advised of the score. At the end of the game it is his responsibility to have the scorecard correctly signed by the players and handed to the appropriate officials.

The marker should position himself at the rear of the jack and to one side of the rink. He should not move, or attempt to move, any bowls or the jack until each player (or skip in the case of sides) has agreed on the number of shots.

Master Bowl   A Master Bowl is one approved by the governing body as having the minimum bias and complying with weight and size as laid down in the Laws of the Game.

Mat line   The mat line is the edge of the mat nearest to the front ditch. It is from the centre of the mat line that any necessary measurements are taken.

Open hand   The side of play, in relation to the position of the jack, that has no, or few, bowls on it compared to the other side.

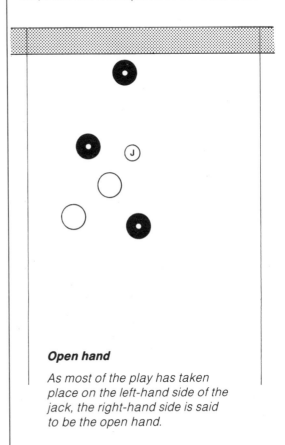

Open hand

As most of the play has taken place on the left-hand side of the jack, the right-hand side is said to be the open hand.

Open jack   A jack that is in full view of the bowler from the mat and not obstructed by a bowl.

Pace of the green   The pace of the green is measured in seconds and is the time a bowl takes from being delivered to coming to rest, approximately 30yd (27·43m) from the mat line.

BOWLS

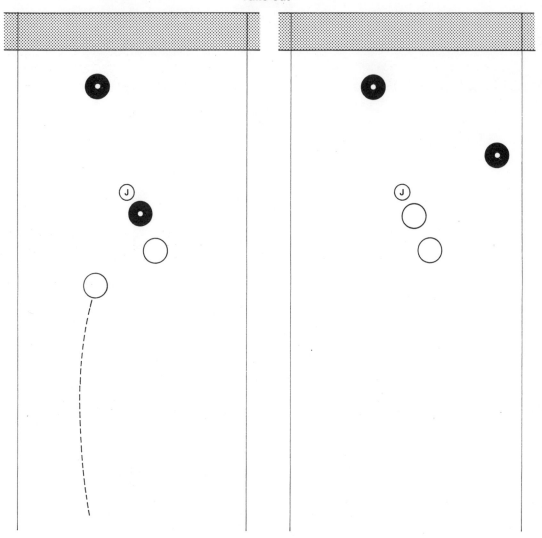

Your running bowl is on course to take out your opponent's bowl that is 'standing shot'. If successful, you could take the shot.

The end result . . . and better than expected; you are now standing with two shots.

***Previous pages:* Flat Green bowls at Mortlake Bowls Club.**

EQUIPMENT · & · TERMINOLOGY

The shot

The following diagrams show the final positions of all bowls at the completion of an end. ('X' indicates a 'toucher'; ● = player A; ○ = player B; ① = jack.)

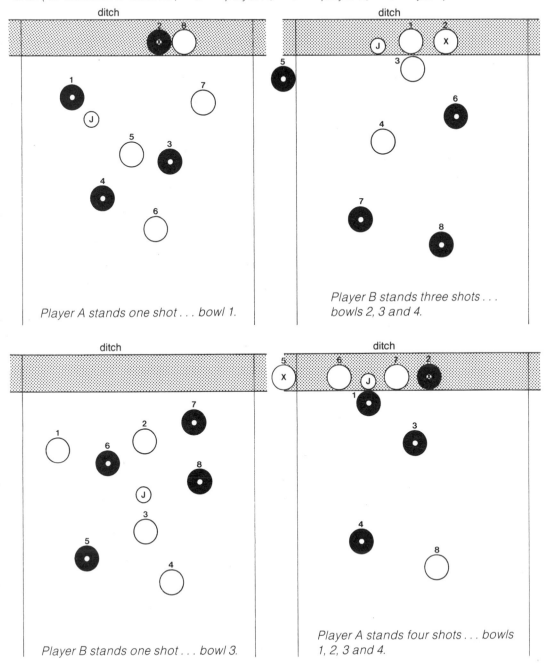

Player A stands one shot . . . bowl 1.

Player B stands three shots . . . bowls 2, 3 and 4.

Player B stands one shot . . . bowl 3.

Player A stands four shots . . . bowls 1, 2, 3 and 4.

BOWLS

Touchers

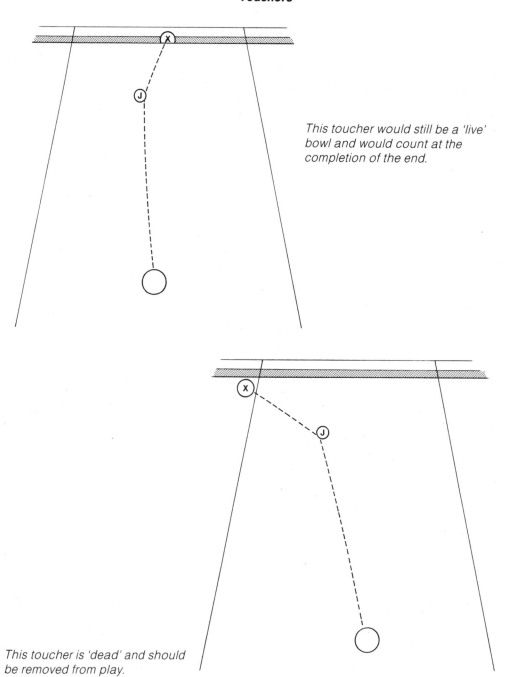

This toucher would still be a 'live' bowl and would count at the completion of the end.

This toucher is 'dead' and should be removed from play.

Pairs   A team consisting of two players, a lead and a skip.

Set of bowls   A set of bowls consists of four bowls all of the same manufacture, size, weight, colour and serial number (if applicable).

Side   A side comprises an agreed number of teams in order to constitute a match.

Skip   The skip is the person in charge of the head on behalf of the rest of his team. He assesses the position of the bowls at the head and advises the next player what shot he should make. The skip is always the last player in a team to deliver his bowls.

Standard Bowl   Each national bowling association has possession of a Standard Bowl which is a duplicate of the Master Bowl.

Take out   A bowl which takes out an opponent's scoring bowl and often replaces it as the scoring bowl.

Team   A team consists of either two, three or four players.

The shot   A shot (or shots) shall be adjudged at the completion of an end and is the number of bowls nearer to the jack than any bowl played by an opponent.

Tie   If at the completion of an end two bowls from opposing sides are touching the jack or deemed to be equidistant from it, the end shall be declared a tie and no points awarded although the end shall count as being played.

Toucher   Any bowl which, in its original course on the rink, touches the jack is a toucher. Even if it touches the jack and then enters the ditch within the confines of the rink, it is still a toucher and is still live.

Trial end   Before the commencement of, or upon the resumption of, a game, the players are allowed to play one trial end each way up the rink.

Triples   A team consisting of three players.

Umpire   The Umpire's duties are:
(a) to check that all bowls comply with legal requirements before the commencement of a game;
(b) to ascertain the width of the rink before the start of a game;
(c) to rule on all decisions as to the distance of the mat from the ditch, and the jack from the mat;
(d) to rule whether the jack and/or bowls are live or dead;
(e) to enforce the Laws of the Game.

All the terms outlined apply to both indoor and outdoor Flat Green bowls, but the Crown Green game has some terms that are unique to its own game and they are as follows:

TERMINOLOGY –
CROWN · GREEN · BOWLS

Land   A player is said to have 'found his land' when he likes playing to a particular part of the green.

Referees   The role of the referee is to see that the game is carried out strictly in accordance with the Laws of the Game. He must also resolve any dispute not catered for in the Laws. His decision is final.

Round pegs   Any jack delivered with its bias complementing the slope of the green will take the path of a sweeping wide arc. This is known as a round peg mark.

Running bowl   A running bowl is a bowl that is on its journey towards the jack. This may be a little obvious but the expression is

BOWLS

A round peg

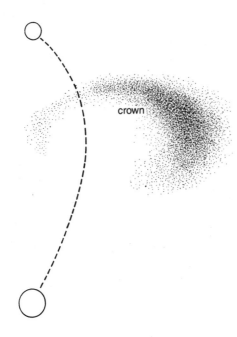

The bias of the jack and slope of the crown help exaggerate the arc of the jack's delivery – a 'round peg' delivery.

used quite often in the Rules Clinic on pages 51–54 and it is therefore best to define it at this stage.

Scorers   The scorers, one representing each player (or pair), shall sit together and check their score cards at the end of every five ends to signify agreement. It is the responsibility of the player (or pair) winning the end to indicate to the scorers how many shots have been won.

Set of bowls   A set of bowls in Crown Green bowling consists of two bowls of equal weight and size. In all forms of Crown Green bowling, each player delivers only two bowls.

Setting a mark   The player who delivers the jack 'sets a mark', and it is the object of all players to get their bowls as near the mark as possible. To set a mark the jack must come to rest anywhere on the green. If it . does come to rest but the nearest point of the jack to the centre of the footer is less than 62ft 4in (19m) then it is not a mark and the jack must be delivered again.

Still bowl   A still bowl is a bowl that has come to rest . . . obvious you are thinking, but, like the running bowl, the term will crop up quite often in the Rules Clinic later in the book.

Straight pegs   The opposite to a Round Peg . . . it is when the jack is delivered with the bias played towards the slope of the green thus counteracting the slope.

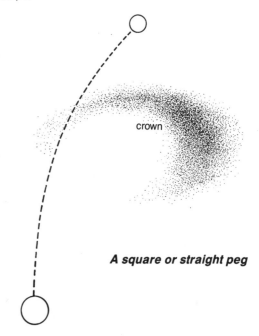

A square or straight peg

The bias of the jack is played towards the slope of the crown, thus counteracting its effect.

We are nearly ready to go. But before you get your mat or footer out, and get ready for action, it is worth having a further and closer look at the bowls used and the effect bias has on them. All three games use the same bowls.

THE · BOWLS –

A · MORE · DETAILED · LOOK

Bowls, as already mentioned, are made out of Lignum Vitae, rubber or composition. The rubber bowl is the least popular of the three.

Lignum Vitae is a very dense and heavy timber grown in the West Indies and on the north coast of South America and it has been used in the manufacture of bowls for more than 200 years. If you buy a brand new set of Lignum Vitae bowls it should be pointed out that they shrink slightly and suffer an initial weight loss in their first season of between $1\frac{1}{2}$–2oz (42–56gm). Additionally, if you leave them in a warm place – in a car or by the side of the green, in hot weather – they will crack. They are best stored in a cool, slightly damp place.

Composition bowls, contrary to belief, are not a new innovation but have been manufactured for more than fifty years for use in countries with warm climates where Lignum Vitae bowls would warp or crack.

Shortly after World War I there was a shortage of Lignum Vitae and an Australian, W. D. Hensell, manufactured the first rubber bowl, thanks to the co-operation of the Dunlop Rubber Company. In 1930 Hensell and his son Ray developed the first 'Henselite' plastic bowl from a phenolformaldehyde compound. The same compound is used as the basis for today's composition bowls.

Composition bowls have the advantage over their wooden counterparts of not warping, cracking, or losing their weight and shape. Climatic conditions do not affect them and they do not require waxing like the Lignum Vitae bowls.

Dimensions and weights have already been outlined on page 15, but it is worth looking at the weight-for-size scale as laid down by the International Bowling Board. Most manufacturers work to this scale when producing bowls.

If a bowl was perfectly round it would travel in a completely straight line along a flat green. Completely round bowls would reduce the element of skill which biased bowls provide. How, for example, could you get your bowl around another bowl that had come to rest in front of the jack? You couldn't, and that is why biased bowls were introduced.

Bias is imparted by shaping the running sole of the bowl, and not by loading it with lead as people often assume. This bias causes the bowl to travel in a curved path.

WEIGHT-FOR-SIZE · SCALE

Size No.		0	01	1	2	3	4	5	6	7
Diameter	mm	118	119.5	121	122.5	124	125.5	127	128.5	130
	in	$4\frac{5}{8}$	$4\frac{11}{16}$	$4\frac{3}{4}$	$4\frac{13}{16}$	$4\frac{7}{8}$	$4\frac{15}{16}$	5	$5\frac{1}{16}$	$5\frac{1}{8}$
Medium Weight	kg	1·24	1·28	1·32	1·36	1·41	1·47	1·52	1·53	1·58
	lb–oz	$2–11\frac{1}{2}$	2–13	$2–14\frac{1}{2}$	3–0	$3–1\frac{3}{4}$	$3–3\frac{3}{4}$	$3–5\frac{3}{4}$	3–6	$3–7\frac{3}{4}$
Heavy Weight	kg	1·28	1·32	1·36	1·41	1·46	1·52	1·58	1·58	1–58
	lb–oz	2–13	$2–14\frac{1}{2}$	3–0	$3–1\frac{3}{4}$	$3–3\frac{1}{2}$	$3–5\frac{1}{2}$	$3–7\frac{3}{4}$	$3–7\frac{3}{4}$	$3–7\frac{3}{4}$

Before you deliver your first bowl it will pay to understand what bias is and how it is measured.

Bias

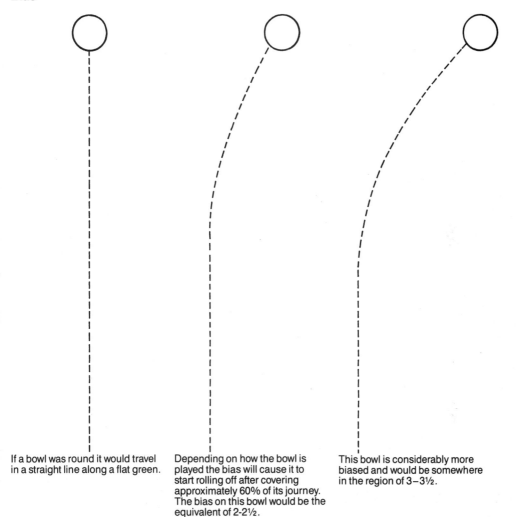

If a bowl was round it would travel in a straight line along a flat green.

Depending on how the bowl is played the bias will cause it to start rolling off after covering approximately 60% of its journey. The bias on this bowl would be the equivalent of 2-2½.

This bowl is considerably more biased and would be somewhere in the region of 3–3½.

The greater the bias, the greater the path of the curve. The amount of bias is measured against a Master Bowl as approved by the International Bowling Board. In the Flat Green game no bowl can have a bias less than the Master Bowl. All bowls are tested and stamped by the manufacturer and must be re-tested every fifteen years to ensure that they still comply. You are not allowed to alter the bias of your bowl, that can only be done by an official tester.

In the Crown Green game, since the jack is biased to a standard bias of 2 most bowls are made with the same bias to enable the bowler to follow the line of the jack.

What exactly is bias? There is no mathematical formula for calculating it

All set for the next delivery!

because the condition of the playing surface or shape of the bowl can affect its running. The expression 'Bias 3', 'Bias 2' etc., are figures that have been arrived at by trial and error and by experimentation, rather than by any magical mathematical formulae.

Prior to 1871 the testing of a set of bowls was unheard of and, as bowls were made by hand, it was impossible for bowls in a set to match each other. But in 1871 Thomas Taylor of Glasgow patented the first machine for accurately shaping bowls, and also constructed a testing table to compare the bias on different bowls.

Bowls were delivered down a chute and their level of bias was measured over a standardized distance. The idea was simple and it revolutionized the game.

Taylor graded his bowls between bias 1 and 5 and in 1893 the Scottish Bowling Association adopted the No. 3 bias as the standard bowl.

The Crown Green authorities experimented with Taylor's grading and decided that No. 2 was not quite strong enough, while No. 3 was too strong. They requested that No. 2 should be made somewhat stronger and when this had been done it became known as 'Bias 2 Full' and that today is the bias on all standard Crown Green jacks.

Leading bowlers will have more than one set of bowls, particularly in the Crown Green game, in order to accommodate the varying greens. On fast greens lighter, unpolished bowls are more popular because they tend to come to rest quicker than heavier bowls. On damp and heavy greens a bowl weighing around 2lb 14oz (1·31kg) is often popular. Don't forget that weather conditions are an all-important factor determining the pace of a green . . . not only today's weather conditions but those of yesterday. It may be nice and hot today but was it raining yesterday? (More than likely if you live in Britain!) In that case the green will be playing slower than normal. All these factors must be taken into account when making your choice of bowl.

To identify which side of the bowl the bias is on, look for two discs, or other distinguishing marks, one on either side of the bowl. The smaller of the two indicates the side of the bias.

Ultimately the choice of bowl always comes down to your own preference. Whatever you feel comfortable with, and providing you are regularly achieving good distance and accuracy with it, then that is the bowl suited to your game. One thing to remember: a new set of Lignum Vitae bowls can lose weight and slightly change shape during the season. So, if you are playing with such a set of bowls and, towards the latter half of the season, you note a change or deterioration in your game, that could well be the answer – your bowls have lost weight! In which case you should take them to an approved tester.

SUMMARY
THE · PRINCIPAL · DIFFERENCES · BETWEEN · FLAT · GREEN · & · CROWN · GREEN · BOWLS

There are many differences between the two codes, but the main ones are:

(1) The playing surfaces are different. The green is completely flat in the Flat Green game but in Crown Green bowls there is a crown at the centre of the playing surface.

(2) The Flat Green game is played in lanes, whereas any part of the green in the Crown Green game can be used.

(3) Crown Green bowlers use two bowls each; Flat Green bowlers use four.

(4) A biased jack, which has a standard bias, is used in Crown Green bowls. The jack is not biased in the Flat Green game.

(5) Crown Green bowls are normally lighter and smaller than their Flat Green counterparts. Flat Green bowls tend to have a much greater bias.

THE
RULES

The object of all forms of bowls is to get more of your own bowls nearer to the jack then those of your opponent(s). You score one point for each bowl that is nearer the jack. That sounds nice and easy doesn't it? To be honest it is . . . well, in theory. But, as with many games, bowls has its idiosyncrasies and we will look a little closer at the rules of our three games. Let's start with . . .

FLAT · GREEN · BOWLS
(OUTDOOR · AND · INDOOR)

Flat Green bowls is played as either singles, pairs (two players per side), triples (three per side) or fours (four per side).

In **Singles** each player has two, three or four bowls depending upon the rules of the competition or as previously agreed between the players. Normally each player has four bowls.

In a **Pairs** match, again two, three or four bowls are used by each player in accordance with the tournament rules, but four is the normally accepted number, and is adopted at major championships.

A **Triples** match at championship level involves each player delivering three bowls, but they can, in other circumstances, deliver only two each. If three each are used,

eighteen bowls can be on the rink at any one time.

In a game of **Fours,** because eight players are participating at the same time, each player has only two bowls.

The method of scoring in each end is as described in the introduction to this chapter, but the duration of a game varies from competition to competition. For a friendly game in your local park you can decide beforehand how long your game will last – perhaps the first to reach a certain figure, over a specific number of ends, or until the park-keeper comes and asks for his bowls back because your hour is up!

As a guideline, the duration of games in major championships are as follows:
Singles: The first person to reach twenty-five shots is the winner (scoring shots in excess

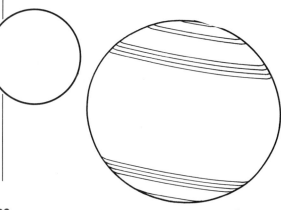

of twenty-five do not count). Singles matches under the EBA jurisdiction, however, are only to twenty-one up.

Doubles: These shall consist of twenty-one ends, the scores of both sides determining the result. If the competition is such that a winner has to be declared, an extra end or ends will be played until such a winner is found.

Triples: These shall consist of eighteen ends. Like doubles, if the match is drawn an extra end or ends are played to determine the winner.

Fours: These are played over twenty-one ends with extra ends being played if the competition necessitates finding a winner.

Before you actually start to play you are allowed to play a trial end each way up the rink. If your game has been carried forward from a previous day, or resumed after a delay, you are still allowed your trial ends.

Right, so you now have the 'feel' of the green, let's get started.

The two players toss a coin to decide who shall have the option of playing first. In the case of a match involving two or more per side, the opposing skips toss.

At the beginning of the first end the player making the first shot shall place the mat lengthwise on the centre line of the rink with the front edge of the mat 6ft (1.84m) from the ditch. Once play has commenced in any end the mat must not be removed until the completion of the end.

The player who delivers the jack must make it travel at least 70ft (21.35m) in a straight line from the front of the mat. The EBA stipulate a minimum distance of 25yd (21.35m).

If the jack comes to rest less than 6ft (1.84m) from the opposite ditch it shall be

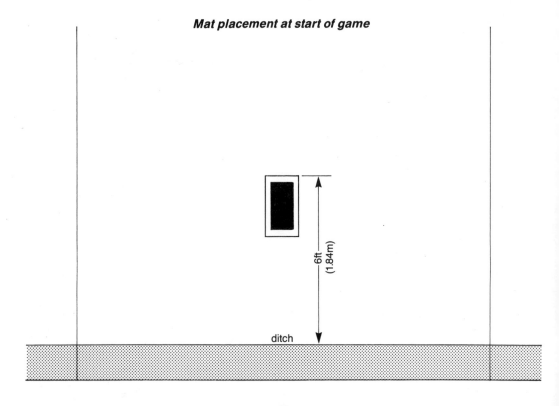

Mat placement at start of game

6ft (1.84m)

ditch

THE · RULES

Correct positioning of the jack

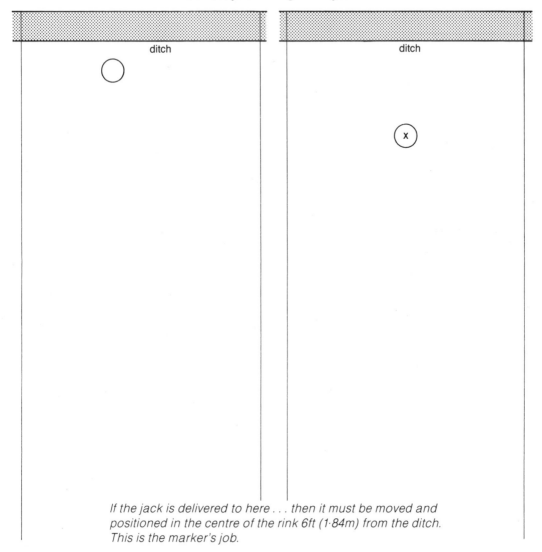

If the jack is delivered to here . . . then it must be moved and positioned in the centre of the rink 6ft (1·84m) from the ditch. This is the marker's job.

moved to a mark at that distance from the ditch and in the centre of the rink.

Once the jack has been successfully and correctly positioned, the players in turn and alternately deliver their bowls with the intention of getting more to finish nearer the jack than those of their opponent(s).

The winner of the first end, and each subsequent end, positions the mat at the start of each new end and delivers the jack to commence the next end. After the first end, the mat must be not less than 6ft (1.84m) from the rear ditch and not less than 76ft (23.16m) from the front ditch. (EBA

Subsequent mat placement

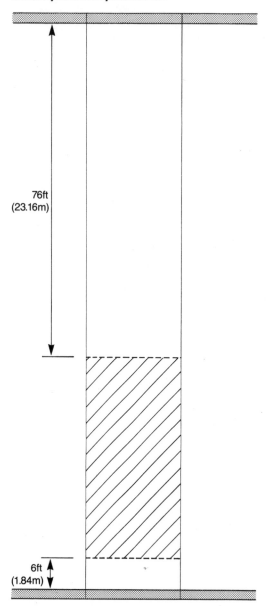

76ft
(23.16m)

6ft
(1.84m)

After the completion of the first end the front of the mat can thereafter be positioned anywhere in the shaded area at the start of all subsequent ends provided it is centred in the middle of the rink.

figures are 6ft [1.84m] and 27yd [24.69m]).

It is permissible for your bowl to touch another bowl, whether it be your own or your opponent's, or even the jack. Any bowl that makes contact with the jack is called a 'toucher' and still counts even if it subsequently goes in the ditch within the boundary of the rink.

A game is completed when the appropriate score, or number of ends, have been completed as outlined above. If an extra end is required, the two opponents or skips toss a coin to decide who plays first and if any further ends are required, a toss of a coin shall once more determine who plays first.

The playing of **INDOOR BOWLS** is no different from Flat Green bowls, and while pairs, triple and fours are played, the most popular game is singles. To accommodate the more 'instant' appeal of television, many televised indoor championships are played over a number of sets with a pre-determined number of ends or points comprising one set. For example, the 1987 World Indoor Championship final at Coatbridge was played over the best-of-nine sets and the first player to reach seven points won a set. England's Tony Allcock beat team-mate David Bryant in a classic six-hour contest: 0-7, 7-6, 7-3, 3-7, 5-7, 7-6, 1-7, 7-5, 7-2.

CROWN·GREEN·BOWLS

In all games of Crown Green bowls each player has only two bowls. You never see triples or fours in the Crown Green game, but pairs is a regular feature, particularly mixed pairs.

The basic principle is the same as Flat Green bowls . . . you have to get one or more bowls nearer the jack than your opponent does.

At the commencement of a game the first

THE · RULES

Position of footer

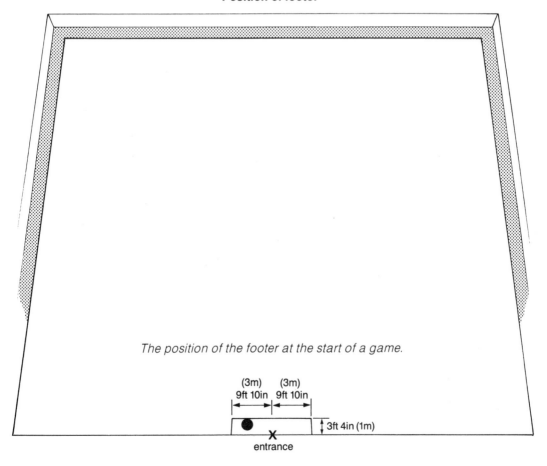

The position of the footer at the start of a game.

person to play, known as the leader, must place the footer within 9ft 10in (3m) of the entrance to the green and 3ft 4in (1m) from the edge of the green. It is from there that play commences. He can deliver the jack, to any part of the green he wishes, but it must travel at least 62ft 4in (19m) from the footer. Once the jack has been delivered and a mark set, play continues with each player delivering a bowl alternately. At the completion of each end, and with the score calculated, the footer is placed where the jack came to rest. The winner of the previous end then plays first but can move the footer within 3ft 4in (1m) from its position.

The game continues until a player (or pair) has reached a pre-determined number of points; twenty-one is the normal but occasionally the game is played until one player (or pair) reaches thirty-one, or even forty-one.

Because Crown Green bowls is not played within the confines of a rink and is played in any direction across the green, congestion quite often occurs. Because of that, take note of where other matches are taking place and do not play your jack towards an already congested part of the green.

RULES CLINIC

FLAT · GREEN · BOWLS
(OUTDOOR · AND · INDOOR)

Is a jack dead if it goes in the ditch?

No, providing it comes to rest within the confines of the rink.

What happens if the jack, when delivered, goes outside the confines of the rink on either side or into the ditch?

It is returned and your opponent delivers the jack but **you** must deliver the first bowl to it once it has been correctly delivered.

If the jack is in the ditch, can a live bowl that comes in contact with it be classed as a toucher?

No.

If a bowl comes to rest close to the jack but without touching it and later falls over on to the jack, is it still a toucher?

Yes, providing it falls over before the next bowl has been delivered or, if it is the last bowl of the end, falls over within thirty seconds of coming to rest.

How do you indicate which bowl or bowls are touchers?

With a suitable chalk mark.

Sometimes it may not be possible to mark a toucher because any interference may cause it to fall over or move. What happens in that case?

The two skips, or opponents in a singles game, agree which ball is a toucher and mark it at the earliest opportunity. After each end is completed you should remove chalk marks from all touchers.

Are there two mats on every rink?

Yes, one at each end of the rink. Once the final bowl of an end has come to rest, or become dead, the mat should be picked up and placed beyond the face of the rear bank. When the next end commences from the opposite end of the rink the other mat, which is also placed beyond the opposite bank, is used.

RULES · CLINIC

What is the penalty if I play a shot with a foot neither on nor over the mat as per the Laws of the Game?

It constitutes a foot-fault and the umpire may, after giving a warning, have the bowl stopped and declared dead.

But what happens if, after a foot-fault, the head is disturbed?

The non-offending player has the option of: (a) having the head replaced as near as possible to the original position; (b) leaving the head as altered, or; (c) declaring the end dead.

Foot faults

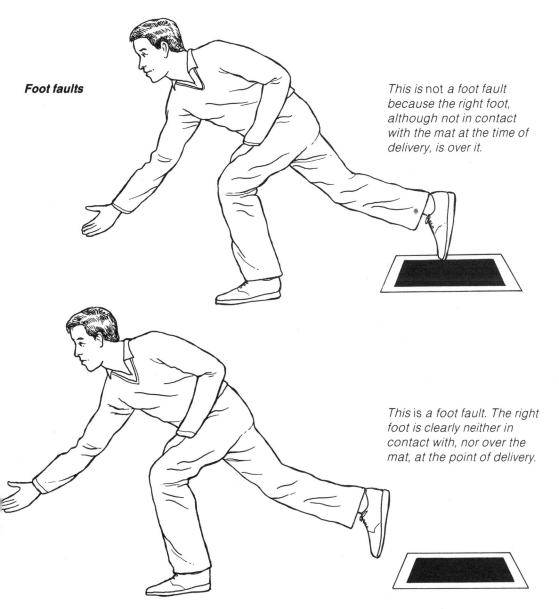

This is not *a foot fault because the right foot, although not in contact with the mat at the time of delivery, is over it.*

This is *a foot fault. The right foot is clearly neither in contact with, nor over the mat, at the point of delivery.*

BOWLS

In and out of the rink

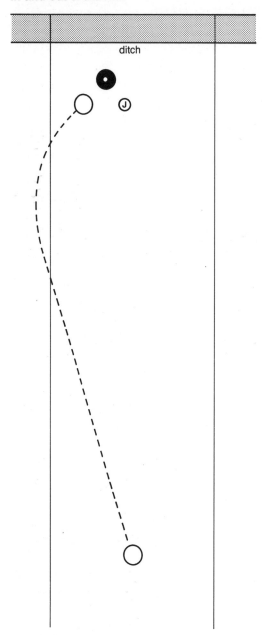

ditch

J

*A bowl can leave the rink and re-enter it.
It remains a live bowl.*

Can a bowl rebound from the face of the bank onto the green?

Yes, but it only remains a live bowl if it is a toucher. If not it is dead. A toucher can also rebound into the ditch off the face of the bank and still be live.

If, in a moment of forgetfulness, I pick up a toucher that is in the ditch, believing it to be dead, can I just put it back and apologize?

You can certainly apologize, but you can't just put it back.

If a player interferes with any live bowl before the completion of the end the opposing skip, or opponent in singles, can insist on either: (a) the bowl being restored as near as possible to its original position; (b) letting it remain where it subsequently comes to rest; (c) declaring the bowl dead or; (d) declaring the end dead. As there are quite a few options open to your opponent the message is simple . . . don't have too many fits of amnesia on the bowling green.

Can a bowl be rolled with such bias that it leaves the side perimeter of the rink and re-enters it?

Yes . . . but make sure you don't interfere with an adjacent head.

There must be cases when bowls or the jack are moved inadvertently by an outside party, other than the players concerned in the end?

Yes there are, and the Laws of the Game make provisions for such occurrences.

In the main, the opposing skips, or opponents in singles, should agree on the replacement of the bowls, or jack, interfered

England's Tony Allcock puts a query to the marker during a match in the 1987 UK Indoor Championship.

BOWLS

Forcing the jack out of position

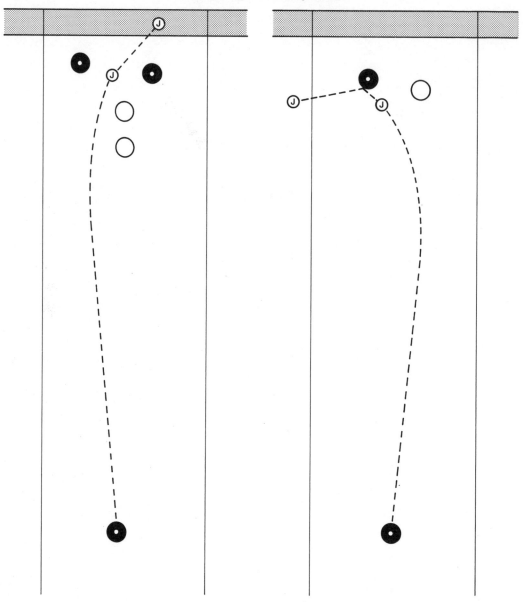

Jack forced into ditch –
end still live.

Jack forced out of rink –
end dead.

with and they should be replaced as near their original position as possible.

If a bowl is moved whilst in the process of being marked a toucher, it should be replaced, either by an opponent or by the umpire or marker if one of them moved the bowl.

If a toucher in the ditch is displaced by a dead bowl, the toucher should be replaced to its original position.

What happens if a bowl makes contact with the jack and forces it outside the boundaries of the rink?

It is declared dead, and the end is declared dead. It shall be replayed in the same direction unless both skips, or opponents, agree otherwise. The jack would be dead if it went out of the side boundaries of the rink, over the bank, or rebounded from the bank to a distance of 61ft (18·59m) from the front edge of the mat. The EBA ruling states 22yd (20·12m).

After a dead end who delivers the jack?

The right remains with the player who delivered it originally.

In what order do players deliver their bowls in a game of fours?

The lead players shall deliver their two bowls alternately, the second players their two and so on, until the skips deliver the last four bowls, again alternately.

I am the last to play in an end and hold the one, or possibly more, winning shots. Do I have to deliver my last bowl?

No.

How long can a player wait at the completion of an end before the winning shot (or shots) is announced?

Half a minute. If you have a bowl that looks like rolling over nearer to the jack, it is worth the wait.

What happens if a non-toucher rebounds off the face of the bank and disturbs the head?

The head shall be restored as near as possible to its original formation, and the offending bowl removed from the head.

What happens if I play out of turn or play the wrong bowl?

If you play out of turn the opposing skip can stop your bowl in its travel or, if too late, decide to leave the new head as it is or declare the end dead. If you play your opponent's bowl by mistake, it shall be replaced, when it has come to rest, by the correct bowl.

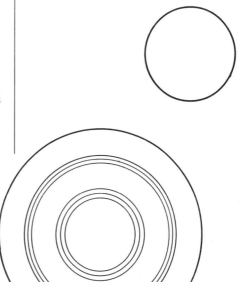

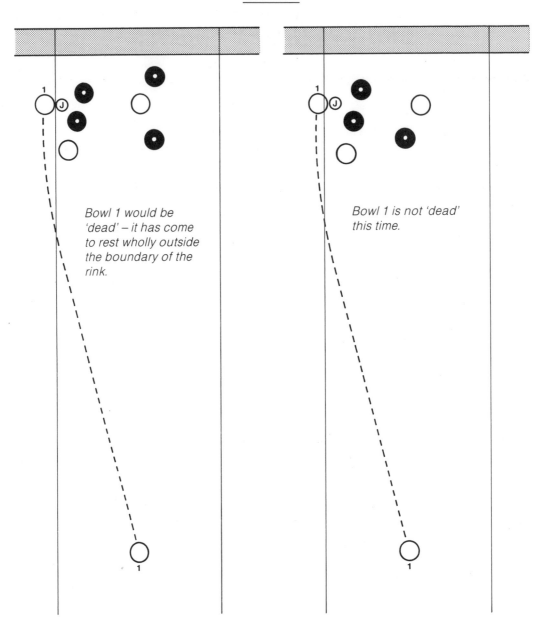

Bowl 1 would be 'dead' – it has come to rest wholly outside the boundary of the rink.

Bowl 1 is not 'dead' this time.

If the jack has been driven to the side of the rink, can I deliver my bowl so that it travels outside the boundary of the rink to reach the jack?

As we have already said – yes. You can deliver a bowl that goes out of your rink, but it must return to the rink in order to be a live bowl. Therefore, if you play to a jack on the boundary of the rink, your bowl must return to its own rink to count. It may be that it touches the jack but comes to rest wholly outside the rink. It is therefore dead and must be removed.

CROWN · GREEN · BOWLS

Can I deliver the jack with my right hand and bowl with my left?

No. Whichever hand you deliver the jack with must also be the one that delivers your bowls. Any bowl played with the wrong hand shall be stopped by the referee and played again . . . correctly. If you do it again during the course of the game, the bowl will be declared 'dead' and will not count.

What happens if it is my turn to set a mark but it is deemed 'not a mark' for one reason or other?

Then your opponent attempts to set a mark, but **you** must then play first towards the jack. If, however, he fails to set a mark then you can have another go. Irrespective of how many attempts the pair of you have at setting a mark, it will always be you who plays first towards it because that was your honour at the start of the end.

Who objects to the legality of a mark – one of the players or the referee?

Either you or your opponent, depending upon who was setting the mark. Objection to a mark must be made **after** the first bowl has been delivered. If the mark is subsequently found to be good the jack and bowl remain in position. If you are objecting to a mark made by your opponent **after** you had failed to make a successful mark (or vice versa) then you must object **before** you play your first bowl.

As the jack has a bias on it, can I withhold from my opponent information concerning the bias I put on the jack?

No. What a bad sport you are for asking such a question! You must, according to the Laws, give your opponent the opportunity of seeing which bias you play the jack with, and of watching its course from a point near the footer.

What happens if a good mark has been made but, during play, the jack is struck off the green?

The end is deemed to be over and neither player shall score. Play resumes with the jack being played to commence the next end at a point 3ft 4in (1m) from the point where it left the green. The same player sets the new mark.

Can I change the jack or my bowls during a game?

Yes, but only if the referee considers either so severely damaged that they are unplayable. You can't change your bowls because you are on a losing streak and feel a new set might change your luck . . . believe me, it will have nothing to do with luck anyway!

Is it permitted to follow a running bowl across the green?

Yes, but you must not approach within 3ft 4in (1m) of the bowl, and you must not follow it in such a manner that your opponent's view is obstructed. You must not impede or accelerate your bowl's progress. Any infringement will result in the bowl being taken out of the end and any future offence will result in the game being awarded to your opponent.

I know I can deliver a bowl so that it blocks the path of an opponent's bowl, but can I do this by delivering my bowl just in front of the footer?

Yes, providing your bowl travels 13ft (3m) from the footer.

BOWLS

When measuring the distance between bowl and jack, where exactly are the measurements taken to?

The nearest points between the two objects. A special measure is used but in some cases when it is difficult to ascertain which is the nearest bowl to the jack, calipers are used. But these cannot be used if one of the bowls, or jack, being measured is in the ditch.

Measuring

When measuring between the jack and a bowl the nearest point between the two objects is used: A – B in the diagram. A tape measure is an essential piece of bowls equipment.

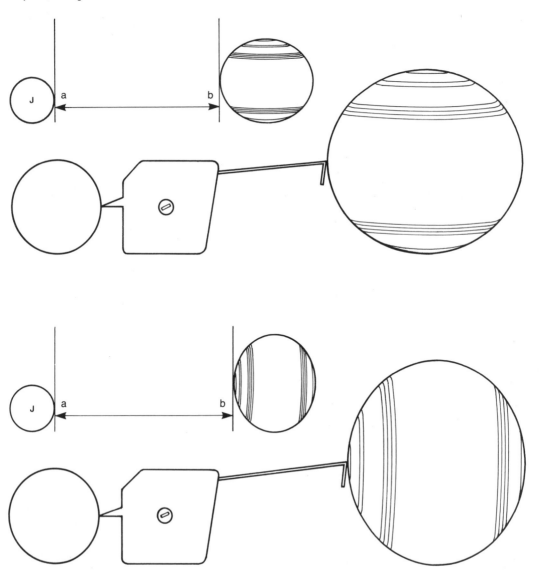

Can I call for a measure at any stage during an end?

Yes, but you forfeit any bowls you have remaining. Normally the measure takes place at the completion of an end and must be carried out by the referee or measurers specifically employed for the purpose of measuring. Whoever makes the measure must not place either thumb or finger on bowl or jack when making a measure.

What happens if my bowl or jack hits a bowl or jack from an adjacent game, or vice versa?

Crown Green bowling can get very congested at times, which is why you have to be alert as to where play is going on around you. There is nothing worse than seeing a tense and exciting finish to an end being ruined by a bowl from another end disturbing your head. Inevitably 'accidents' will happen and the Laws make provisions.

   If a running bowl is impeded in any way, other than by either player, it must be played again. If a running jack or bowl is in danger of hitting a still jack or bowl in another head, it should be stopped and returned to be replayed. If a still bowl is disturbed by a running bowl, running jack, or person from another game then the bowl should be replaced as near to its original position as possible.

What happens if I should pick up and play my opponent's bowl by accident?

It shall be deemed a dead ball and returned to its rightful owner to deliver. You forfeit one of your bowls as a penalty. If a jack or bowl is displaced as a result of playing the wrong bowl then it shall be replaced as near its original position as possible.

If a player takes up the footer after playing a bowl which has then to be replayed, what happens?

The footer should be replaced as near to its original position as possible. If you remember **not** to pick up the footer until the completion of an end you won't have any such problems.

Is a bowl deemed to have been played if it falls out of my hand?

If, after taking up your position on the footer, the bowl falls out of your hand and you cannot retrieve it without leaving the footer then it is a dead bowl and is taken out of the end. If you can retrieve it you may continue playing with it. Long-armed players have a distinct advantage with this rule . . .

Serves you right for dropping it!

If my bowl touches the jack and then goes off the green, is it still in play?

No. Unlike Flat Green bowls where it would still count, it is a dead bowl in the Crown Green game.

Can I stand behind the jack while my opponent is delivering his bowl?

My! You really are unsportsmanlike aren't you? Fortunately the Laws do state that you must not stand directly behind the jack or obstruct the view of an opponent. Even without this Law most bowlers would, through the laws of commonsense and decency, not hinder their opponent thus.

If the jack is played off the green by a bowl is it still 'live'?

No. If the jack leaves the green after a mark has been set the end is declared over and another commences with the same player setting the mark.

A bowl is dead if it goes off the green but what happens if it is prevented from going off the playing surface by an object in the channel surrounding the green?

Sorry, but it is still dead. However, if the green is well kept there is very little likelihood of this happening.

Obstruction

If the bowl is prevented from going off the green by a 'foreign' body, it is deemed to be dead.

Measuring the distance between a bowl and the jack.

TECHNIQUE

GETTING · STARTED –
GRIP · AND · STANCE

The first thing you have to do is learn how to hold the bowl. Before doing this you should make sure that your bowls are the right size and weight for you. If they are the right size they should fit snugly into the space made when you join your two thumbs and middle fingers together. As to weight, that is a personal preference, but as we have said earlier, the condition of the green often affects such a choice.

There are two standard types of grip, the claw grip and the cradle grip.

With the claw grip the bowl sits near the base of the fingers and the little finger and

How to find the right sized bowls

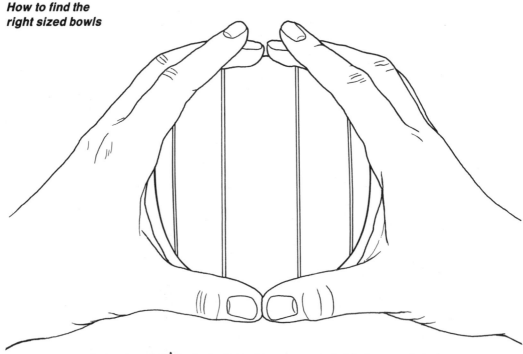

A simple way to find what sized bowls are suitable for your hands. Join your thumbs and middle fingers together. The bowl should fit snugly in the space created.

Grip

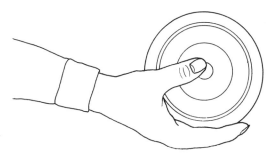

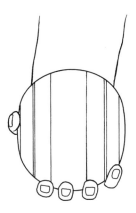

The claw grip: *When firing the thumb should be moved nearer the top of the bowl for extra grip.*

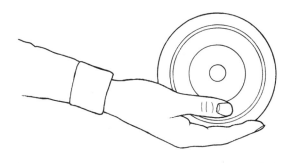

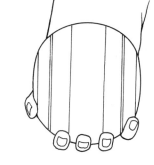

The cradle grip:

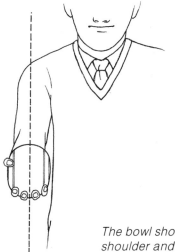

The bowl should be held level with your shoulder and should remain level through the backswing and delivery.

Delivering the jack

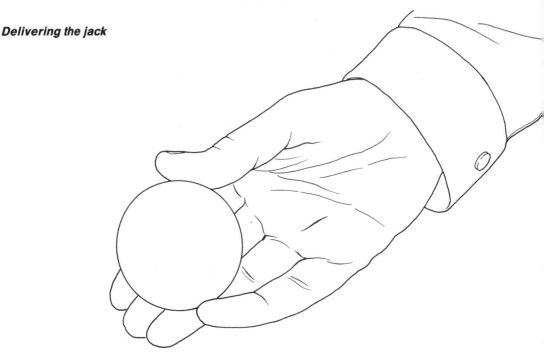

When delivering the jack in flat green bowls, don't hold it in the palm of your hand – you will get more accuracy if you hold it like this.

thumb provide extra support to stop the bowl slipping at the moment of delivery. If you are firing (see page 63) the thumb should be moved nearer the top of the bowl to give a firmer grip.

When using the cradle grip the bowl sits more in the palm of the hand with the thumb positioned lower down the side of the bowl. This type of grip is not suitable if you have small hands, or larger bowls.

Crown Green players, because their bowls are generally smaller, tend to hold the bowl with the thumb on one side of the bowl and little finger on the other (known as thumb peg and finger peg, depending upon which side the bias is on).

There are two recognized stances, the crouch and the upright stance. Choice is a personal one and indeed some players develop a mixture between the two. It is

impossible to tell you how you should position yourself at delivery. I can detail the two stances mentioned and then you can sit in front of the television and watch the top players in action and it will bear little relation to what you have just read.

The important thing to remember with stance is to make sure than you are comfortable, that your backswing is fluent, and you keep your balance. It is also useful to develop a good follow through after delivering your bowl; this eliminates any possibility of jerking the bowl at the point of delivery.

As we have already learned, the object of a game of bowls is to get your bowl(s) to finish nearer the jack than your opponent's. It sounds easy doesn't it? But don't you believe it!

Stance

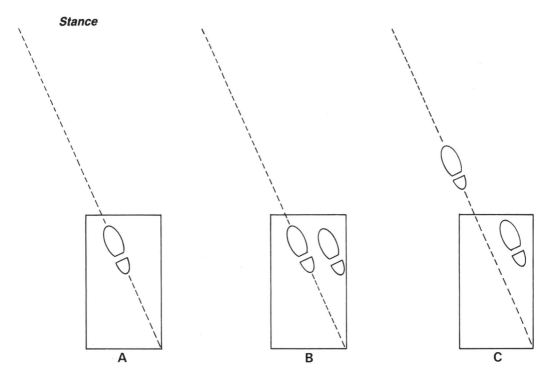

A   B   C

*Correct positioning of your feet is important. This is how they should be positioned when: **A** lining-up the shot; **B** when taking up the stance; and **C** at the moment of delivery. The broken line indicates the point of aim.*

LINE · AND · LENGTH

No matter which game you are playing, the principal two skills are the same – line and length. Line is delivering an accurate bowl to the jack or pre-determined destination, while length is the playing of it with sufficient weight to reach its destination.

Let's first of all look at the effect of line in the **FLAT GREEN AND INDOOR** games.

As we have seen, the jack is not biased and after being delivered is centred in a straight line from the bowler's mat. Thereafter it is the player's skill that counts in finding the appropriate line which his bowl should take to finish near the jack.

Finding the line is achieved by delivering his bowl on either the forehand (with the little finger on the bias side of the bowl) or the backhand (with the thumb on the bias side of the bowl). This is assuming the player is right-handed. Obviously, the opposite would apply for a left-handed player.

Then, depending upon the strength of his woods (the amount of bias) the player must pick his line accordingly, knowing that heavily biased bowls will need more green than a less biased bowl.

Unfortunately not every bowl you deliver will be a toucher, and it is therefore very important to concentrate on the line bowled by both yourself and your opponent to enable you to make any necessary

Finding the right line

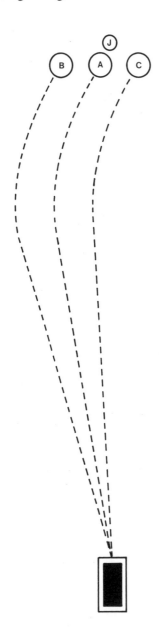

Three identical bowls delivered with the same weight. Only A has found the right line.

adjustments to subsequent deliveries.

The **CROWN GREEN** game takes on a different aspect as the jack (or block) has a standard bias, and it can be delivered to any part of the green – within the rules that is (see page 43).

Since most players use woods of similar bias to the standard jack, you would think, therefore, that it is easy to bowl good woods every end. Don't be fooled. Nothing is that easy!

In Crown Green bowls every green is different so that home-based players have a big advantage with their knowledge of the green. They know the good parts of the green to deliver the jack to, and know those parts of the green that will confuse their opponents.

The jack can be delivered with either the finger or thumb on the bias side, known as finger peg or thumb peg. The player must advise his opponent(s) which method of delivery he has adopted, merely by saying 'finger' or 'thumb'. From here on it comes down to one thing, CONCENTRATION.

Watch carefully the land the jack takes, and try in your own mind to form a mental picture of that particular line. Less experienced players will look for something on the green over which the jack travels, for example a dark piece of grass, a clover, a bare patch, or anything else which catches the eye. Other players try to spot a distant object as their target. It may be a bed of flowers, a tree, a bench around the green or, again, anything that catches the eye. But the more experienced you get, the more easily will a mental picture of the line of delivery build up.

To aid your concentration, it is a good tip, if you are delivering the jack, to hold your bowl in your other hand so that you do not have to take your eye off the line when you bend down to pick up your bowl.

Having noted the line, your bowls should now be sent on the same line as the jack, but also realizing that if you miss the land by anything like a foot on a severe round peg

TECHNIQUE

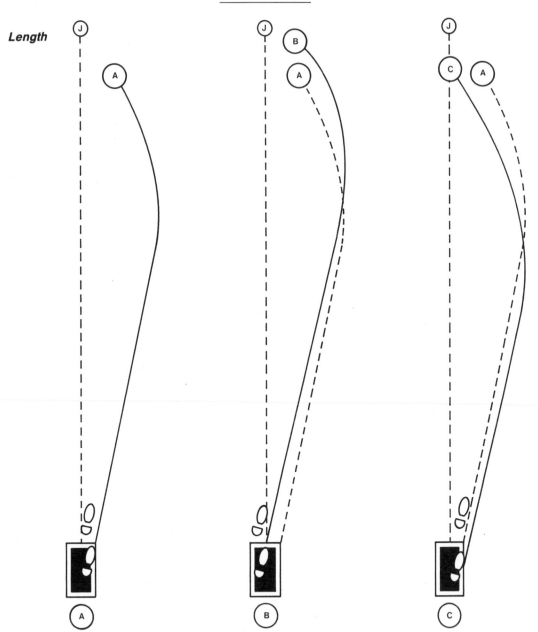

Length

Three forehand shots played along the same line, but with different weights. A is a good bowl, but not a winner because by playing with extra weight, as in B, it is possible to go round the back of A. (Note the shift of feet and point of delivery in shot B). To get inside bowl A you would have to play the same line, but with less weight, as in C. Note again the feet positions and point of delivery.

mark, you could end up a very long way away from the jack.

It should be noted that if the jack is sent by, say, finger peg, the woods need not be sent the same way, but it is easier to follow the line of the jack. More confident players, and players on their 'home' green, will often turn their wood over and play the opposite way if they do not fancy their chances of winning the end by playing the same line as the jack.

Right, that is line, now for the downfall of most bowlers – length. The question of length for both Flat Green and Crown Green bowls can be described in one word, 'feel'.

On more than one occasion you will hear a bowler come off the green and say: 'I just couldn't get a length', referring to the fact that his deliveries were either too far through the jack (overplayed) or too short (underplayed). This is where 'feel' comes into the game.

No matter whether you are bowling to a jack 22 yards (20m) or 70 yards (64m) away, you must have the right 'feel' and, sadly, it is impossible to put into words how you find length. Only experience will tell you that. It is all down to the player's own feel for the woods and ability to make the necessary adjustments to turn a losing shot into a winning one.

All bowlers, whether they be Flat Green or Crown Green, have a favourite distance to which they would prefer to bowl, and most of them know, or soon find out, their opponent's weaknesses. In Crown Green bowls, most good players will tell you to learn to play from corner-to-corner first. Bowl your corners well, so it is said, and the rest of your game will look after itself.

If you are constantly playing too short with your first bowl, try aiming at a point just behind the back of the jack for all subsequent bowls, and rectify accordingly with your second bowl. As in every other game, practice makes perfect – and you will certainly never play good bowls without plenty of it!

The draw

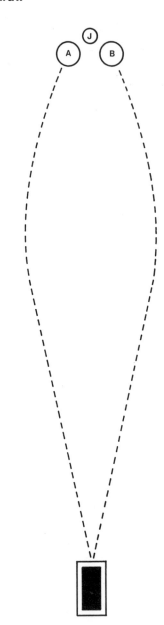

The draw, the most common shot in bowls. A represents the backhand draw and B the forehand.

Firing

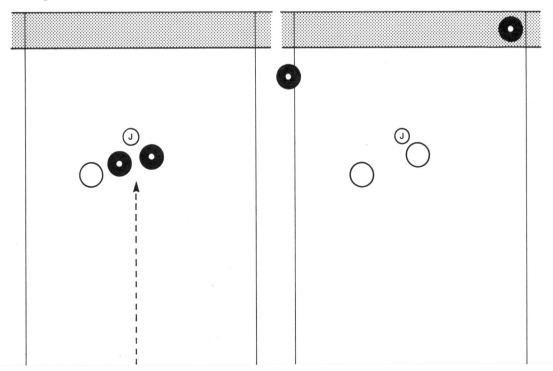

In this situation you are standing two shots down and unable to draw to the jack on the forehand or backhand. The firing shot is your only option . . .

. . . the result: from being two down you stand holding two shots.

THE · SHOTS

The draw

The draw is the most common shot in bowls. It can either be played on the forehand or backhand, which have been explained on pages 22 and 26.

Firing

To be a good competitive player in Flat or Crown Green bowls a player must learn how to fire at the head (known as striking in Crown Green bowls).

The intention is to disturb the head to which a player does not think he can draw a winning bowl, and thus hopefully turn a losing situation into a winning one, or alternatively to kill the end.

Never be afraid to play the firing shot, it may just turn out to be a winning shot, but make sure you have no other options first.

Playing a blocker

The other extreme to playing a bowl with weight is to play it short directly, or near enough in line between the mat and the jack, thus blocking your opponent's line. This is assuming you hold shot . . .

Don't forget that to be a live wood, however, your bowl must travel the minimum distance from the mat in accordance with the rules.

Blocker

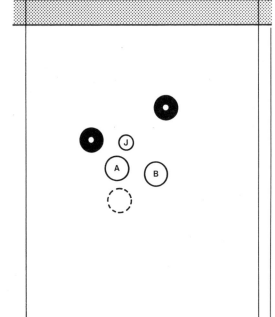

In this head you are nicely positioned, holding one shot. A blocker played in front of bowl A would further hinder your opponent. As things are, a draw to the jack is difficult and a blocker would make firing difficult, because a fired bowl could possibly ricochet off the blocker.

The back bowl

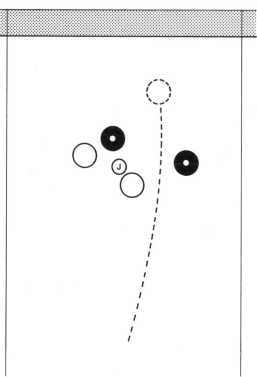

You are holding shot, but your opponent is left with three options. He can draw on the backhand to the jack, trail the jack out of the head, or fire. As insurance against the latter two you would be well advised to play a back bowl.

The back bowl

Another bowl which you will find yourself playing quite often is the back bowl. It is used more often in the Flat Green game than in the Crown Green game and is a useful shot to carry in your repertoire when you are holding shot and suspect your opponent may try to disturb the head, or trail the jack out of the head. A back bowl is useful insurance against such an occurrence. It is also useful to have a back bowl in case the jack ends up in the ditch; it could be a winning bowl – in Flat Green bowls that is.

Playing the trail

The trail is a difficult shot to play but if played correctly is effective and impressive. The bowl makes contact with the jack and the two travel away from the head maintaining contact all the time. In the Flat Green game, if the bowl can be trailed into the ditch then the player making the shot cannot be beaten as his toucher cannot be bettered.

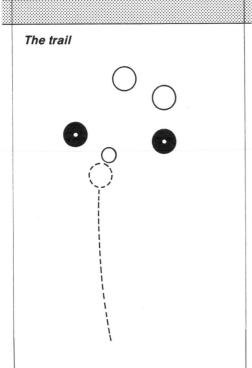

The trail

Despite being two shots down you are in a good position – if you can play a successful trail, that is. With a trail you can 'pick up' the jack with your bowl and 'carry' it towards your two back bowls, possibly giving you three shots.

Throwing a wobbler!

Occasionally, and particularly if you are a novice, you will see your bowl travel in such a way that it 'wobbles'. This is because it is not travelling on the running part of the bowl. The cause – you had your little finger too far up the side of the bowl. The Crown Green term for this is 'cobbled'.

Practice

The good thing about bowls practice is that you can do it on your own. Furthermore it does not have to become boring and tedious. If you are a Flat Green player, the best practice is by constantly drawing your four bowls to the jack but varying the length to get used to the 'feel' of the extra (or shorter) length. The same applies to the Crown Green bowler, but keep selecting different lands to play to, and draw your bowls to the jack.

There can be no better place to finish this book than on the subject of practice, because that is the only way you can expect to become a better player.

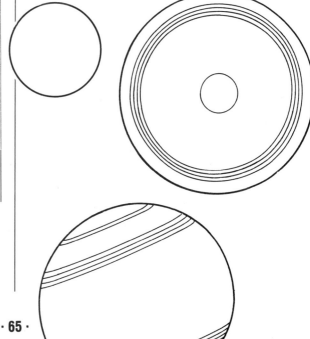

BUILDING · AN · END

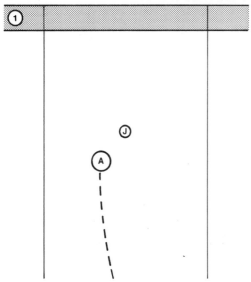

A nice draw for openers. Already your opponent has had the backhand draw shot made difficult, if not impossible.

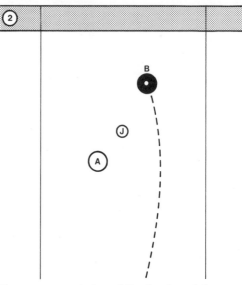

Your opponent played the forehand draw, but overplayed it, and you still hold shot.

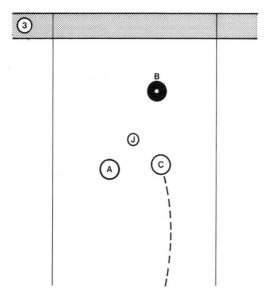

You now hold two shots as a result of a good forehand draw. Now your opponent is in trouble . . .

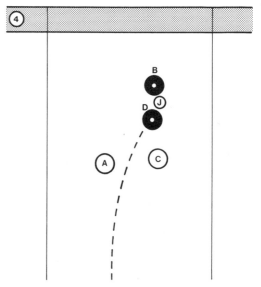

. . . but not for long. He found a gap between A and C to draw on the backhand and trail the jack to bowl B. Now you are down by two shots . . .

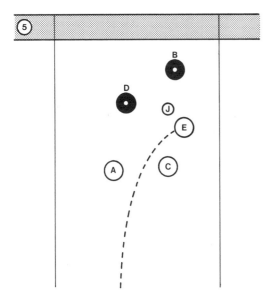

Firing would have been one way out of the predicament, but that would probably have killed the end. An accurately played backhand draw has put you back holding shot after taking bowl D out, which in turn took bowl B out.

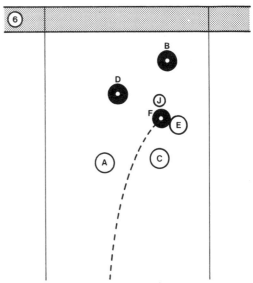

There is still a lot of bowls left in this end, and your opponent has put the pressure back on you with a perfectly weighted backhand.

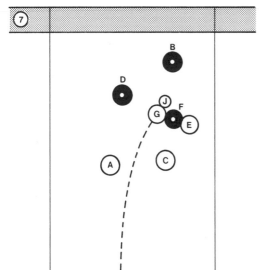

Now things are really warming up. A magnificent backhand on to the jack has given you shot – and your opponent problems.

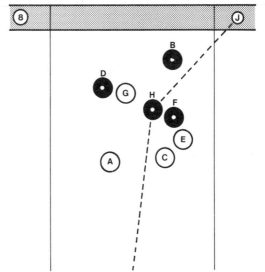

Your opponent was left with no alternative but to fire, which he did successfully and killed the end. Now you have to start all over again . . .

CROWN · GREEN · BOWLS:

HOW · WOULD · YOU · TACKLE · THE · SITUATION?

We are going to look at three hypothetical situations which could very easily arise during a game. We will look at the possible ways of tackling each situation.

Situation A:

Your opponent has two woods (A and B) counting. A is 1ft (30·48cm) behind the jack and in a direct line from the mat.
B is a mere 6in (15·24cm) to the right of the jack. Your first wood has pegged away short and to the left of the end. All three woods have been delivered finger peg. What are your alternatives with your final wood? Your options would be:

(a) Be optimistic and bowl thumb peg, hoping either to push your own bowl closer to the jack or possibly take out your opponent's bowl B, leaving your own bowl in its place.

(b) You could try and bowl a perfect length finger peg wood which would probably have to rest on the jack to count. You are asking for great accuracy taking this option.

(c) Put a bit of running into a finger peg bowl and attempt to dislodge bowl B. If it doesn't take out B then there is a chance of picking up the jack and running it out past your opponent's bowl A.

(d) Take a gamble and strike. . . . The result may be in the laps of the gods, but with any luck you could take out bowl B and be just one shot down . . . at least it's an

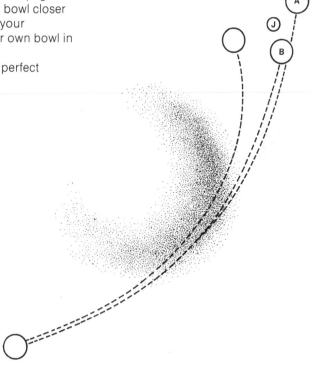

What would you do with your final wood?

improvement. If you are very lucky B might take out A leaving you to count the shot, or possibly two shots. As a third alternative, the strike may take the jack off the green leaving the end dead.

Well! what would you do . . . it's not easy is it?

Situation B:

Your opponent is counting two shots again. (What's happened to you? You used to be better than this!) Bowl A is 6in (15·24cm) short of the jack and his second bowl, B, is 3ft (91·4cm) short. Both are in a direct line

from the mat. The jack was delivered on a straight thumb peg mark along the base of the crown. Your first wood has sailed 4ft (1·22m) past the jack. How are you going to salvage *this* situation?

Your choices:

(a) Turn your bowl over and play a perfect finger peg bowl using the bias of the bowl and the crown to take your own bowl past the two counting woods of your opponent.

(b) You could try and cut your loss to one shot by playing a thumb peg with a touch more land, enabling you to get past bowl B.

(c) Since a thumb peg strike is no good because B is in the way it could be worth trying to strike with a finger peg delivery, but on a much tighter line than in (a) above. After passing bowl B your bowl would either take out A or the jack, or push A on to the jack and that, in turn, on towards your back bowl.

They get harder don't they? Well, what would you do?

Even more of a problem . . .

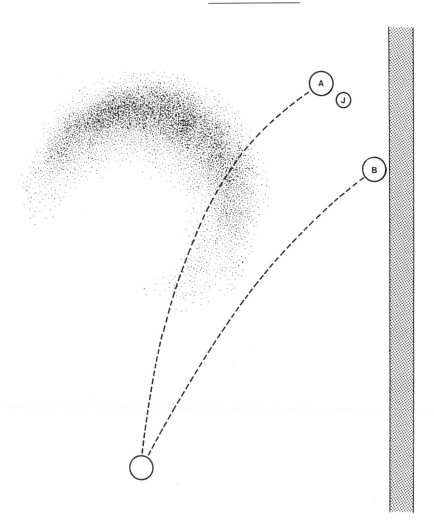

Situation C:

Now for a pressure situation. The score is 20 across (20-20), and you both need one more point to win. Let's add some more pressure: there is a £1000 first prize. So you had better make the right choice this time . . .

You and your opponent have both played one bowl. As it stands you, having delivered first wood A, have the advantage and stand game. You played a swinging thumb peg to 1ft (30·48cm) to the left of the jack. Your opponent played on a tighter line than the jack and has pegged away to finish 6ft

A real pressure situation.

(1·83cm) from its intended target and close to the ditch. Now for the hard part. With standing game shot, you have to decide what to do with your final wood.
The possibilities:

(a) Bowl a short wood to within about 10yd (9·14m) of the mat so as to obscure your opponent's vision and land in case he decides to use forcing tactics.

BOWLS

The same problem from another point of view . . .

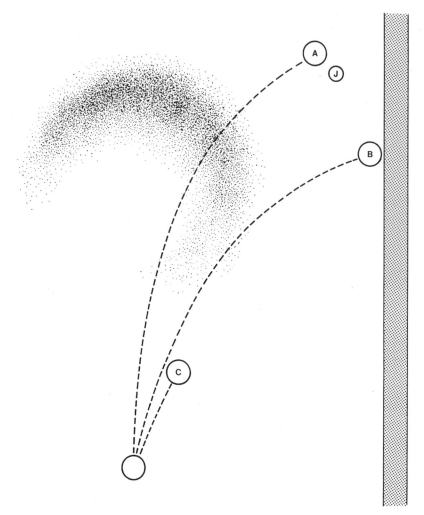

(b) You have the scope to bowl a second wood close to the jack to make your count two. But in doing that you give your opponent a bigger target to rest his bowl on or to strike at. Providing you leave enough room between your two bowls it will reduce the size of his target, and if he is successful in getting one of your bowls away there is a good chance you will still stand shot. If you give him a large target to aim at he can take both your bowls out.

Which option would you take? Both are good options, but the choice is yours.

Let us look at this situation again, but this time you are B (the second player) and your opponent has chosen to play the shot as in option (a). You are in a bit of a mess. His bowl has landed 10yd (9·14m) away from the mat and in a direct line between the mat and jack. What are you going to do?

TECHNIQUE

The ideal outcome.

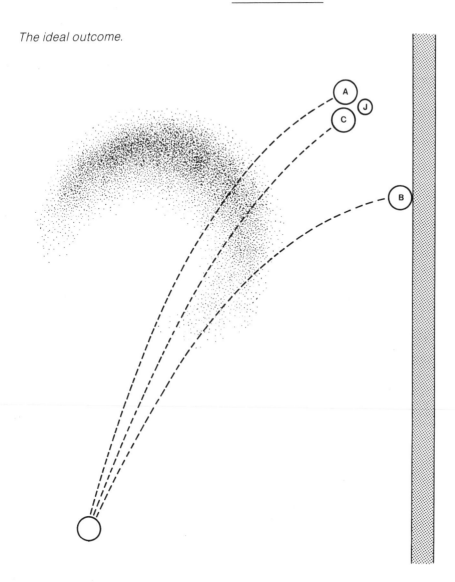

(c) A finger peg straight strike is out of the question – the road is blocked. But you could strike thumb peg knowing that the short wood is not an obstacle. With the natural elements of the green and the bias of the wood you would, if you hit the correct land, take out the winning bowl or possibly take out the jack and, as the head is near the ditch, force a dead end.

(d) With the short wood in your way you have another option – play the perfect ball and rest it on the winning bowl A, or better still, on the jack. After all, you know the land by now.

Had your opponent, instead of sending the short wood, sent a good second to count two, your situation would be verging on the desperate . . . don't forget, there is £1000 at stake!

BOWLS

Here are two further choices:

(e) Strike finger peg straight at the jack, hopefully knocking it off the green (but that is only a temporary respite – you will have to go through all this agony in the next end!). With this course of action there is the chance you will hit your opponent's bowl B and force him to cannon into A and take both his bowls out.

(f) as in (d), you can always play the perfect thumb peg wood.

. . . the choice is yours. And that just about sums up bowls . . . the choice *is* yours. You will find yourself in dozens of different situations per game, each with two or three possibilities. You have to make not the right choice, but the choice *you feel is right.* There are times when it pays off, there are times when it goes hopelessly wrong. But bowls is no different to any sport in that respect.

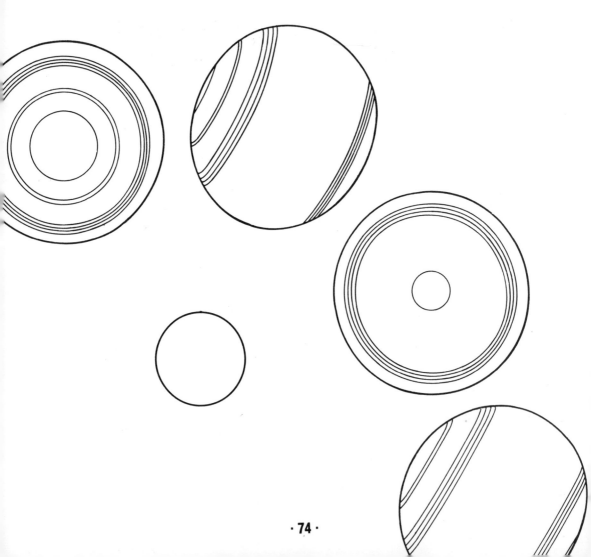

USEFUL
ADDRESSES

INTERNATIONAL · BOWLING · BOARD –
FULL · MEMBERS

American Lawn Bowls Association
11660 SW King George
King City
Oregan 97224
United States of America

Australian Bowling Council
Box Q293
Queen Victoria Post Office
Sydney 2000
Australia

Canadian Lawn Bowling Council
785 Alder Avenue
Sherwood Park
Alberta
T8A 1VI
Canada

English Bowling Association
Lyndhurst Road
Worthing
West Sussex
BN11 2AZ
England

Irish Bowling Association
212 Sicily Park
Belfast
BT10 0AQ
Northern Ireland

New Zealand Bowling Association
PO Box 65–172
Mairangi Bay
Auckland 10
New Zealand

Scottish Bowling Association
50 Wellington Street
Glasgow
G2 6EF
Scotland

South African Bowling Association
15 Keyes Court
Keyes Avenue
Johannesburg
South Africa

USEFUL · ADDRESSES

Welsh Bowling Association
48 Pochin Crescent
Tredegar
Gwent
NP2 4JS
Wales

Zimbabwe Bowling Association
PO Box 4523
Harare
Zimbabwe

OTHERS

British Crown Green Bowling Association
14 Leighton Avenue
Maghull
Liverpool
Merseyside
L31 0AH
England

English Bowling Federation
62 Frampton Place
Boston
Lincolnshire
PE21 8EL
England

English Indoor Bowling Association
290a Barking Road
London
E6 3BA
England

English Women's Bowling Association
2 Inghalls Cottages
Box
Corsham
Wiltshire
England

English Women's Indoor Bowling Association
'Jadran'
8 Oakfield Road
Carterton
Oxford
OX8 3RB
England

David Corkill in action during the 1987 UK Indoor Championship. He finished runner-up to Tony Allcock.

RULES CLINIC
INDEX

INDEX